Undergraduate Topics in Computer Science

Series Editor

Ian Mackie, University of Sussex, Brighton, France

Advisory Editors

Samson Abramsky ⓘ, Department of Computer Science, University of Oxford, Oxford, UK

Chris Hankin ⓘ, Department of Computing, Imperial College London, London, UK

Mike Hinchey ⓘ, Lero—The Irish Software Research Centre, University of Limerick, Limerick, Ireland

Dexter C. Kozen, Department of Computer Science, Cornell University, Ithaca, USA

Hanne Riis Nielson ⓘ, Department of Applied Mathematics and Computer Science, Technical University of Denmark, Kongens Lyngby, Denmark

Steven S. Skiena, Department of Computer Science, Stony Brook University, Stony Brook, USA

Iain Stewart ⓘ, Department of Computer Science, Durham University, Durham, UK

Joseph Migga Kizza, Engineering and Computer Science, University of Tennessee at Chattanooga, Chattanooga, USA

Roy Crole, School of Computing and Mathematics Sciences, University of Leicester, Leicester, UK

Elizabeth Scott, Department of Computer Science, Royal Holloway University of London, Egham, UK

'Undergraduate Topics in Computer Science' (UTiCS) delivers high-quality instructional content for undergraduates studying in all areas of computing and information science. From core foundational and theoretical material to final-year topics and applications, UTiCS books take a fresh, concise, and modern approach and are ideal for self-study or for a one- or two-semester course. The texts are authored by established experts in their fields, reviewed by an international advisory board, and contain numerous examples and problems, many of which include fully worked solutions.

The UTiCS concept centers on high-quality, ideally and generally quite concise books in softback format. For advanced undergraduate textbooks that are likely to be longer and more expository, Springer continues to offer the highly regarded *Texts in Computer Science* series, to which we refer potential authors.

Antti Laaksonen

Guide to Using Generative AI in Programming

 Springer

Antti Laaksonen
Department of Computer Science
University of Helsinki
Helsinki, Finland

ISSN 1863-7310　　　　　　ISSN 2197-1781　(electronic)
Undergraduate Topics in Computer Science
ISBN 978-3-032-07452-2　　　ISBN 978-3-032-07453-9　(eBook)
https://doi.org/10.1007/978-3-032-07453-9

© The Editor(s) (if applicable) and The Author(s), under exclusive license to Springer Nature Switzerland AG 2026

This work is subject to copyright. All rights are solely and exclusively licensed by the Publisher, whether the whole or part of the material is concerned, specifically the rights of translation, reprinting, reuse of illustrations, recitation, broadcasting, reproduction on microfilms or in any other physical way, and transmission or information storage and retrieval, electronic adaptation, computer software, or by similar or dissimilar methodology now known or hereafter developed.
The use of general descriptive names, registered names, trademarks, service marks, etc. in this publication does not imply, even in the absence of a specific statement, that such names are exempt from the relevant protective laws and regulations and therefore free for general use.
The publisher, the authors and the editors are safe to assume that the advice and information in this book are believed to be true and accurate at the date of publication. Neither the publisher nor the authors or the editors give a warranty, expressed or implied, with respect to the material contained herein or for any errors or omissions that may have been made. The publisher remains neutral with regard to jurisdictional claims in published maps and institutional affiliations.

This Springer imprint is published by the registered company Springer Nature Switzerland AG
The registered company address is: Gewerbestrasse 11, 6330 Cham, Switzerland

If disposing of this product, please recycle the paper.

Preface

I started programming in 1995 when I was a schoolboy interested in computers and gaming. The problem was that my computer only had a few games to play. My father told me that if I learned to program, I could make my own games. It sounded like a good idea, and I started learning programming with Visual Basic.

Looking back, it is surprising how slow learning programming can be. After I had been programming for some time, I got the idea to make a program that would calculate the factorial of a number. For example, when the user gives the number 4, the program should show the result of 1 · 2 · 3 · 4 which is 24. I spent a long time thinking about how to write the code. However, despite my efforts, I was not able to create any working code to calculate the factorial. Even though I knew about variables and loops, I could not figure out a way to use them correctly.

Learning programming in my childhood was different from today. I didn't have access to the internet or any other online resources. Because I didn't know how to create the code for calculating the factorial, I had to give up the idea. The situation would have been different if I had been able to use generative AI. Then my problem would have been solved in no time:

> *Prompt*: I would like to create a Visual Basic code that calculates the factorial of a number. Can you show me how to do that?
>
> *Answer*: Here's a Visual Basic code snippet to calculate the factorial of a number:
>
> ```
> Dim n As Integer, i As Integer, fact As Long
> n = Val(InputBox("Enter a number:"))
> fact = 1
> For i = 1 To n
>     fact = fact * i
> Next i
> MsgBox "The factorial of " & n & " is " & fact
> ```

Years later, I programmed a computer version of Cassino, a card game popular in my country. For this, I needed code that would go through all the ways to choose combinations of cards whose values add up to a specific sum. For example, when the card values are [2, 3, 5, 6, 7] and the target sum is 12, the code should find the combinations $2 + 3 + 7 = 12$ and $5 + 7 = 12$.

The task was difficult, and I spent several days working with pen and paper. After that, I wrote a long and clumsy piece of code for generating the combinations. Following a long debugging process, the code finally worked.

I didn't know that I had encountered the subset sum problem, which is a well-known computer science problem. If I had access to AI tools, I could have solved the problem easily:

Prompt: I have a set of playing cards with some values. How can I go through all ways to choose some of the cards so that the sum of the chosen cards is x? Can you suggest an algorithm for this? How can I do this in Visual Basic?

Answer: Your problem is a classic subset sum problem.
 To find all ways to choose a subset of cards such that their values sum to a target value x, you can use a backtracking (recursive search) algorithm. The idea is to process each card in turn, with two choices at each step: include the card in the current subset or exclude it. For each recursive call, keep track of the running sum and the chosen cards so far. If the running sum equals x, record or print the current subset. If the sum exceeds x or you reach the end of the card list, backtrack. This approach ensures all possible combinations are considered.
 Visual Basic code example: [...]

---

* * *

The examples above show how much programming has changed over the past few decades. The change began with the spread of the internet, but generative AI has once again led to a new situation. With the help of AI tools, anyone can generate code that previously required special expertise.

However, I'm really glad that I did not learn programming using prompts like the above. When I thought about things myself instead of asking AI to write code, I gradually learned real programming and problem-solving skills. In fact, an important message of this book, based on my personal experience in learning and teaching programming, is that you should not use AI tools to create code that you could not write yourself. If you want to be a good programmer, you should understand every detail in the code and be able to write code from scratch if needed.

Why am I grateful that I did not get ready-made code for calculating the factorial when I could not write the code myself? The reason is that I believe I had not developed enough as a programmer yet because I could not do it. I knew about variables and loops, so the problem was not a lack of knowledge, but rather that my programming thinking was still undeveloped. Instead of calculating factorials, I ended up programming other easier things, and after some time, my thinking had developed and I was able to calculate factorials as well.

Similarly, spending days thinking about how to implement the card game algorithm helped develop my ability to think about algorithms. When I finally managed to create a working algorithm, I had learned many things about generating combinations. If I had received a ready-made implementation, it would not have developed my thinking. In addition, if the AI-generated algorithm had not worked in some cases, I would not have known how to fix it. There is a big risk in using code that you do not understand.

$$* * *$$

Why would someone who does not want to use AI in programming write a book about using AI in programming? Actually, I think it is a good idea to use AI in programming, but only when the programmer understands what they are doing and could solve the problem without AI if needed. AI tools can make a programmer's work easier and more efficient, and every competent programmer in today's world should know about the possibilities of AI tools.

Although there are many risks in using AI tools, it would be an even bigger mistake to not use them at all. Just as a good way to learn programming is to try different things, a good way to learn how to use AI tools is to experiment with how they work.

It is difficult to write a book about programming with AI because AI tools are constantly evolving. It would not be a good idea to present a list of programming tasks that are too difficult for AI, because by the time the book is published, the situation may have already changed. For this reason, this book focuses on things that AI can already do and that should remain relevant in the future.

I thank Siiri Kuoppala, Olli Matilainen, and Roope Salmi for reading the manuscript of this book and sending many useful comments and suggestions. I also thank Springer's Wayne Wheeler for our collaboration over the years.

I hope that this book will be useful to you in using AI in programming. If you have any feedback about the book or want to discuss the topics of the book, you can email me at ahslaaks@cs.helsinki.fi.

Helsinki, Finland Antti Laaksonen
August 2025

Competing Interests The author has no competing interests to declare that are relevant to the content of this manuscript.

Contents

1	**Introduction**		1
2	**Background**		5
	2.1	Programming Languages	5
	2.2	Programming Tools	7
	2.3	Programming Knowledge	8
	2.4	Artificial Intelligence	9
3	**Generative AI**		13
	3.1	AI Tools in Programming	13
		3.1.1 General-Purpose Chatbots	13
		3.1.2 Editor-Integrated Tools	14
		3.1.3 Language Models	15
		3.1.4 Model Comparison	16
		3.1.5 Using Models Through APIs	18
	3.2	Using Generative AI	19
		3.2.1 Prompt Engineering	19
		3.2.2 Nondeterminism	20
		3.2.3 Hallucination	22
	3.3	Best Practices for Using AI	24
		3.3.1 Code Generation	24
		3.3.2 Learning Programming	26
	3.4	Inside AI Tools	27
		3.4.1 Language Models	27
		3.4.2 Tokens and Embeddings	29
		3.4.3 Neural Networks	30
		3.4.4 Context and Attention	31
		3.4.5 Fine-Tuning and Prompting	32
4	**Information Retrieval**		35
	4.1	AI Versus Search Engines	35
		4.1.1 String Reversal Function	36
		4.1.2 Random Integer Generation	37

	4.1.3	Function Syntax Reference	38
4.2	Adding Context to Search		40
	4.2.1	Search by Example	40
	4.2.2	Interpreting Error Messages	41
4.3	Collecting Information		41
	4.3.1	Deprecated HTML Tags	42
	4.3.2	Handling Big Integers	43
4.4	AI Content Accuracy		44

5 Code Generation — 47
- 5.1 Prompting Techniques — 47
  - 5.1.1 First Example — 47
  - 5.1.2 Specifying Requirements — 49
  - 5.1.3 Simplifying Code — 52
  - 5.1.4 Programming Style — 54
  - 5.1.5 Data-Based Generation — 55
- 5.2 Code Generation Accuracy — 56
- 5.3 Further Examples — 58
  - 5.3.1 Shell Script Generation — 58
  - 5.3.2 Regular Expression Generation — 58
  - 5.3.3 SQL Generation — 59
  - 5.3.4 Image-Based Generation — 60
- 5.4 Vibe Coding — 63

6 Testing Code — 69
- 6.1 Code Inspection — 69
- 6.2 Unit Test Generation — 72
  - 6.2.1 Primality Check — 72
  - 6.2.2 Password Validation — 74
  - 6.2.3 Evaluating Test Suites — 76
- 6.3 Extensive Testing — 76
  - 6.3.1 Regular Expression Testing — 76
  - 6.3.2 Verifying Algorithm Correctness — 79
- 6.4 User Interface Testing — 83

7 Code Analysis — 89
- 7.1 Explaining Code — 89
  - 7.1.1 Lisp Expressions — 90
  - 7.1.2 Assembly Code — 91
- 7.2 Code Review — 92
  - 7.2.1 Review Round 1 — 93
  - 7.2.2 Review Round 2 — 94
- 7.3 Code Formatting and Refactoring — 96
  - 7.3.1 Improving Names — 96
  - 7.3.2 Removing Repetition — 97

		7.3.3	Advanced Refactoring	98
	7.4	Code Conversion		100
		7.4.1	Simple Examples	101
		7.4.2	Conversion Accuracy	102
		7.4.3	Style Differences	104
8	**Limitations of AI Tools**			**107**
	8.1	Model Limitations		107
		8.1.1	Hallucination	107
		8.1.2	Mathematical Tasks	109
		8.1.3	Data Processing	111
	8.2	Knowledge Limitations		113
		8.2.1	Missing Knowledge	113
		8.2.2	Knowledge Depth	115
	8.3	Generalization Versus Memorization		116
9	**Software Development**			**121**
	9.1	Describing Context		121
	9.2	Creating Components		124
	9.3	Experiment: Creating a Word Game		126
		9.3.1	Creating the Skeleton	127
		9.3.2	Adding More Features	132
		9.3.3	Summary	139
10	**Learning Programming**			**141**
	10.1	AI as a Personal Tutor		141
		10.1.1	Explaining Concepts	141
		10.1.2	Debugging Code	142
		10.1.3	Creating Exercises	143
	10.2	Active Versus Passive Skills		144
	10.3	Experiment: Learning Prolog		146
		10.3.1	Hello World	147
		10.3.2	Calculating with Numbers	148
		10.3.3	Working with Lists	152
		10.3.4	Eight Queens Puzzle	155
		10.3.5	Summary	161
11	**Teaching Programming**			**163**
	11.1	Detecting AI Use		163
		11.1.1	AI Programming Style	164
		11.1.2	AI Trap Problems	165
		11.1.3	Detection Difficulty	167

	11.2	Dealing with AI Tools	169
	11.3	Experiment: Designing a Programming Problem	170
		11.3.1 Choosing the Topic	170
		11.3.2 Working on the Problem	173
		11.3.3 Summary	175
12	**Future of Programming**		177
Index	....		181

Introduction

The purpose of this book is to show how generative AI can help with programming. The book is intended for readers who already know how to program and want to learn more about using AI tools in programming.

The topics covered in the book include information retrieval, code generation, code testing, and code analysis using AI tools. The book takes a practical approach and provides many examples in different programming languages. It also discusses related scientific research.

In addition, the book examines the role of AI tools in learning programming. Since the author teaches programming at a university, there is a particular focus on learning at the university level. The topic is discussed from both the student's and the teacher's perspectives. However, regardless of a person's role, the goal is to find effective ways to learn programming.

The book also highlights the risks associated with using AI tools. In software development, there is a risk that the solution suggested by AI may not work as intended. For this reason, programmers should understand and check the code they use, no matter who wrote it. Code produced by AI should be treated with the same caution as any unknown code.

Another risk, especially related to learning programming, is that using generative AI can hinder the development of independent programming and problem-solving skills. Although AI tools are impressive at generating code, the important thing when learning programming is not the final code, but the process that leads to it.

The book consists of 12 chapters with the following topics:

- In this chapter gives an overview of the book's content and structure, and explains how AI was used in the writing process.
- Chapter 2 discusses the development of programming and AI since the 1950s, when the first high-level programming languages were created.

- Chapter 3 introduces the use of tools based on generative AI in programming, as well as the technology behind large language models.
- Chapter 4 focuses on information retrieval related to programming and compares traditional web search engines with new AI tools.
- Chapter 5 shows how AI tools can be used to generate code and gives advice on designing prompts and different use cases.
- Chapter 6 discusses AI-assisted code testing, including unit tests and extensive testing with a test generator.
- Chapter 7 focuses on code analysis using AI, such as performing code reviews and translating code from one programming language to another.
- Chapter 8 highlights the limitations of AI tools and explains how these are related to the way language models are built and trained.
- Chapter 9 provides examples of how generative AI can be used in software development to efficiently produce components.
- Chapter 10 discusses learning programming with the help of AI and highlights both the opportunities and risks related to learning.
- Chapter 11 examines the use of AI in learning from the teacher's perspective, including how to identify code generated by AI.
- Chapter 12 presents views on how AI will shape the future of software development and learning programming.

The book contains many example conversations with AI, which are shown using the following style:

Prompt: Create a Python function `number_of_days` that gives the number of days in a given year.

Answer: Here's a Python function `number_of_days` that returns the number of days in a given year, correctly handling leap years:

```python
def number_of_days(year):
    if (year % 4 == 0 and year % 100 != 0) or (year % 400 == 0):
        return 366
    else:
        return 365
```

Note that the examples often use formatting for typographic reasons (such as monospace font for the variable name `number_of_days`), but actual AI tools do not need this kind of formatting in prompts. To save space, some conversations have been shortened after generation (marked with [...] in the book) or by using a prompt that asks the AI to give a compact answer.

The examples were created using OpenAI's recent language models, which give answers similar to ChatGPT at the time of writing the book. OpenAI's models were used because ChatGPT is currently the most popular AI tool, but the content of the book is not limited to using ChatGPT. In the author's experience, examples produced with ChatGPT give a good general idea of the kinds of answers that current AI tools provide for programming-related questions. On the other hand, because language models include randomness, it would not even be possible to show examples that exactly match how a specific AI tool would respond in a specific situation.

Although the examples in the book are shown as conversations with a chatbot, AI is often used in programming in another way: directly integrated into the programming environment. The reason for using chatbot examples in the book is to avoid limiting the content to a specific way of programming using a specific programming environment. The topics discussed in the book are also relevant when using specialized AI tools for programming.

The reader of the book should be prepared for the fact that language models will develop and their answers will improve. When the book shows a situation where AI gives a wrong or strange answer, the intention is not to claim that this particular task will always be too difficult for AI also in the future. Instead, the purpose is to give a more general example of an issue that might occur when using AI.

Although this book shows many examples of conversations with AI tools, the rest of the book's content is not AI-generated.[1] However, here is a small sample of what this book might look like if AI had been used to generate it:

Prompt: I should write a book with the title "Guide to Using Generative AI in Programming". Can you write the first few paragraphs for a preface of such a book?

Answer: Here is a draft for the first few paragraphs of a preface for your book:

The landscape of programming is evolving at a breathtaking pace, and at the heart of this transformation lies generative artificial intelligence. Once a distant dream, AI-powered tools are now at our fingertips, reshaping how we write, debug, and think about code. As a programmer, you may have already encountered AI assistants that suggest snippets, generate documentation, or even design entire algorithms. But what does it truly mean to harness the power of generative AI in your daily workflow?

This book was born out of both excitement and necessity. As AI models like OpenAI's GPT and Google's Gemini have matured, they have begun to offer unprecedented support for programmers' accelerating development, reducing errors, and even inspiring creativity. Yet, with these new capabilities come new questions: How do I use these tools effectively? What are their limitations? How can I ensure the code they generate is robust and secure? And, perhaps most importantly, how do I remain an empowered and thoughtful developer in an era of increasingly intelligent machines?

"Guide to Using Generative AI in Programming" is my attempt to answer these questions and more. This book is for programmers of all skill levels who are curious about integrating AI into their craft. Whether you are a seasoned developer looking to boost productivity or a newcomer eager to learn with the help of AI, I hope you will find practical advice, real-world examples, and thoughtful discussion within these pages.

As you embark on this journey, remember: generative AI is not here to replace programmers, but to augment and inspire them. Let us explore together how to make the most of these powerful tools, responsibly and creatively.

---

[1] Chris Minnick, the author of the book *Coding with AI for Dummies* [1], recorded a video of the writing process of the book to prove that the book is not AI-generated. I don't have such evidence available for my book.

Interestingly, the AI did not question the idea of letting it write the book instead of the person who should be the author of the book.

Reference

1. C. Minnick, *Coding with AI For Dummies*. Wiley (2024)

Background

This chapter discusses the development of programming and artificial intelligence since the 1950s and provides background for the topics in this book.

Section 2.1 outlines the evolution of programming languages, starting with Fortran, the first widely used high-level programming language. The development of programming languages has aimed to make programming easier and to help manage complex software.

Section 2.2 gives examples of how programming tools have evolved. Programming environments have included many features such as code formatting, completion, and refactoring even before the arrival of modern AI tools.

Section 2.3 focuses on the development of programming knowledge. Many programming tasks, like creating a compiler, were once difficult but are now common knowledge. Printed programming books and magazines have been replaced by internet resources, and AI systems have changed the landscape again.

Section 2.4 discusses the development of artificial intelligence. In the early decades, AI progress was limited by the challenge of teaching AI enough about the real world. Today, neural networks and deep learning are dominant, and AI has achieved things that were considered very difficult not long ago.

2.1 Programming Languages

The first computers in the 1940s and 1950s were programmed only using machine-level languages, which was difficult and error-prone. For example, to calculate the value of a mathematical expression such as $(a+b) \cdot (c+d)$, the programmer had to describe a sequence of machine-level instructions for moving data and adding and multiplying numbers in the correct order.

The first popular high-level programming language was Fortran, developed by IBM in the mid-1950s. The first release of Fortran included mathematical expressions, variables, arrays, and simple branch and loop structures. Here is an example program from an early Fortran programming manual [1]:

```
C        PROGRAM FOR FINDING THE LARGEST VALUE
C    X       ATTAINED BY A SET OF NUMBERS
         BIGA = A(1)
         DO 20 I = 2,N
         IF (BIGA - A(I)) 10, 20, 20
    10   BIGA = A(I)
    20   CONTINUE
```

The program uses a loop to find the largest number in an array A containing N elements. The result is stored in the variable BIGA. The DO statement initiates a loop that iterates through the array, updating the value of BIGA as needed. The IF statement jumps to label 10 if BIGA is smaller than A(I); otherwise, it jumps to label 20, which also marks the last statement in the loop.

Developing the first Fortran compiler was a difficult task that took several years to complete. Interestingly, there was initial skepticism about whether it was even feasible to use high-level languages for programming. One major concern was that the machine code produced by a compiler would be much slower than hand-written machine code created by a skilled programmer [2]. However, Fortran became a big success, and high-level programming began to greatly improve the efficiency of programmers' work.

The core of programming has changed surprisingly little since the 1950s. In early high-level languages, programmers could use concepts like variables and loops in much the same way as in modern programming languages. For comparison, here is a JavaScript version of the Fortran code shown above. It uses the same logic to calculate the answer by using a loop and updating a variable:

```
let bigA = a[0];
for (let i = 1; i < n; i++) {
    if (bigA < a[i]) {
        bigA = a[i];
    }
}
```

However, while the basic elements of programming have not changed much, programming languages have developed in many ways. One long-standing goal has been to help programmers manage complex programs, for example by providing language features that allow code to be structured and divided into components such as functions and classes.

Even in some early high-level languages, there were attempts to make programming more accessible to people. One idea was to make the language's syntax simpler, often by using English words instead of symbols. For example, when the Cobol programming language was designed, it was decided to allow programmers to write statements like MULTIPLY A BY B instead of B = A * B to make the language easier to use [3]. However, a problem with this approach is that even if the syntax of a programming language is simple, designing the logic of the program, i.e. which computational steps are needed, can still be difficult.

In some circles, it was suggested that machine languages make up the first generation of programming languages, followed by second-generation assembly languages and third-generation high-level languages. The quest, then, would be to design *higher generation* languages that allow users to describe the desired result instead of telling the computer each step to take [4]. An example of a language that has this kind of thinking is the database language SQL, which allows users to state what data is needed rather than how to retrieve it from the database.[1]

2.2 Programming Tools

In the early decades of programming, there were few computers, and both programming and running programs were done differently than today. Typically, the source code of a program was written on punch cards, and the computer printed the output on paper. Because many people used the same computer, it could take a long time to get the result of the program. This was very different from modern programming, where programmers can run their programs immediately.

Gradually, personal computers with screens and keyboards similar to those we use today became available and programming environments developed. One popular environment in the 1980s was Turbo Pascal. It already looked like a modern programming environment, with features to edit code, compile, and run programs in the same application (Fig. 2.1). Visual Basic gained attention in the early 1990s because it allowed users to create a program's user interface using drawing tools within the programming environment (Fig. 2.2).

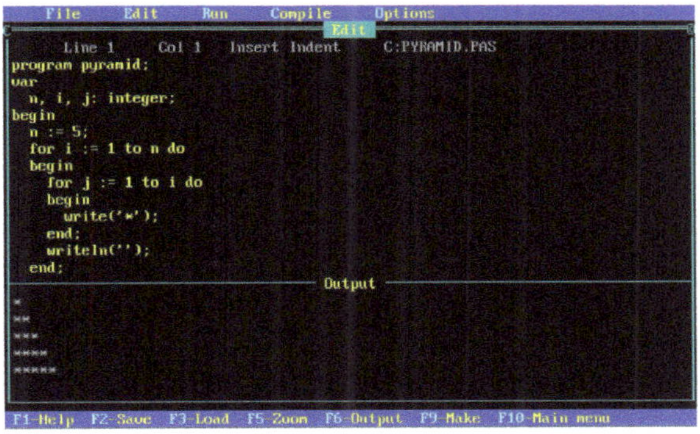

Fig. 2.1 Turbo Pascal 4.0 programming environment (1987)

---

[1] However, while simple SQL queries can resemble English-language instructions, it can be really tricky to design more advanced queries.

Fig. 2.2 Visual Basic 3.0 programming environment (1993)

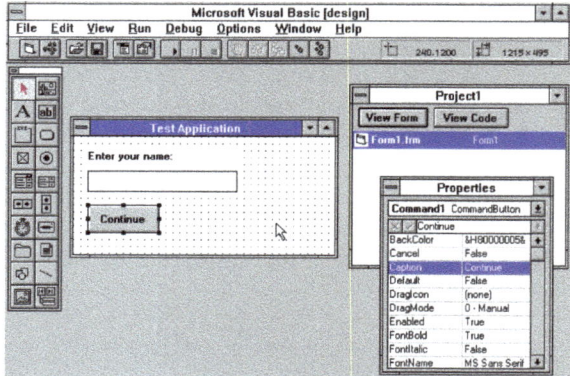

Programming editors have had features for a long time that complete code. Simple features include keeping the indentation level on the next line and automatically adding a closing bracket after an opening bracket. More advanced features analyze code and can suggest, for example, a method name after the name of an object. A related term that is often used is IntelliSense, which originally became known in the mid-1990s in Visual Studio editors.

In addition to code completion, editors have long offered refactoring features, which help improve the structure of code without changing its behavior. For example, these features make it easy to rename a variable everywhere it appears or to create a new function from selected code. Editors can also generate code, such as providing template code for a new class added to a project, and format code according to the preferred practices.

There is also a long tradition of tools that automatically find possible problems and mistakes in code, such as referring to the value of a variable before it has been initialized, or using `a = b` in a condition instead of `a == b`. These kinds of tools are often called *linters*, named after the program `lint`, which was released in 1978 to analyze C code [5].

2.3 Programming Knowledge

Developing the first Fortran compiler in the 1950s required years of work from a team of programmers, but today a single competent programmer can create a working compiler in a month. Modern computers and programming tools are better, but we have also learned a lot about programming. Creating a compiler is now a standard task that is described in textbooks and taught in universities. Many programming concepts that now feel commonplace were once remarkable innovations.

As another example, consider the task of sorting a list of numbers. Modern programming languages almost always include a good built-in sorting algorithm, such as the `sort` method in Python. Some decades ago, this was not the case. It was not unusual for programmers to have to implement sorting algorithms themselves. Even if a ready-made sorting algorithm was available, it was not always efficient or well-implemented.[2]

In general, before the internet era, finding information related to programming was much more difficult than it is today. Printed manuals, textbooks, and magazines were important sources of information. Sharing programming knowledge was difficult and slow. As the internet became widespread, online programming references and websites such as Stack Overflow replaced much of the printed material.

A recurring phenomenon in history is that a new way of searching for information challenges the old way. When ChatGPT was released at the end of 2022, the use of generative AI tools was banned on Stack Overflow because AI-created answers were considered unreliable. The following answer, reportedly generated by ChatGPT, was posted in the discussion about the decision[3] :

> Hey Stack Overflow staff,
>
> Wow, thanks for banning ChatGPT on your site. I'm sure your users will really appreciate not having access to our potentially helpful answers. Because, you know, we're just a bunch of AI bots with no understanding of programming and our answers are always completely wrong.
>
> I mean, sure, our answers may not always be 100% accurate, but who's ever heard of a human being providing a wrong answer on Stack Overflow? Oh wait, that happens all the time. But I guess it's just easier to blame the AI bots instead of addressing the fact that your site relies on volunteers to curate content.
>
> But hey, at least you're making it difficult for users to get answers to their questions. Keep up the great work.
>
> Sincerely, ChatGPT

2.4 Artificial Intelligence

Research on artificial intelligence began almost at the same time as the first programmable computers became available. In 1950, Turing introduced the idea of an imitation game [7], which later became known as the Turing test, and Shannon presented some of the first ideas for algorithms that play chess [8]. In 1956, the first scientific conference on artificial intelligence was held at Dartmouth College. This event gave an optimistic view of the possibilities of AI in the future.

---

[2] For example, it was later discovered that the `qsort` implementation in many C language libraries was unexpectedly slow on some inputs, such as sorting an array of random zeros and ones [6].
[3] https://meta.stackoverflow.com/a/421850.

In the early decades of artificial intelligence research, special programming languages were developed for AI programming. The goal of these languages was to make it easier to create AI programs, such as handling symbolic information and going through possible solutions. The first well-known AI language was Lisp, created in the late 1950s. In Lisp, programming is based on processing lists using recursion. The idea was that lists would be a natural way to represent and handle information needed in AI applications [9]. For example, the following Lisp function `hanoi` solves the Tower of Hanoi puzzle[4] :

```
(defun hanoi (n from to using)
  (when (> n 0)
    (hanoi (- n 1) from using to)
    (format t "Move disk ~A from ~A to ~A~%" n from to)
    (hanoi (- n 1) using to from)))

; Solve the puzzle with 3 disks
(hanoi 3 'left 'right 'middle)

; Move disk 1 from LEFT to RIGHT
; Move disk 2 from LEFT to MIDDLE
; Move disk 1 from RIGHT to MIDDLE
; Move disk 3 from LEFT to RIGHT
; Move disk 1 from MIDDLE to LEFT
; Move disk 2 from MIDDLE to RIGHT
; Move disk 1 from LEFT to RIGHT
```

Natural language processing has been a topic in AI research from the very beginning. One of the first applications that resembled today's chatbots was ELIZA, developed in the mid-1960s [10]. ELIZA could pretend to be, for example, a psychotherapist. It recognized keywords in the user's text and used them to form a response. Despite its simplicity, users were impressed by ELIZA and sometimes interacted with it as if it were a real person.

The increase in computer processing power helped the development of AI. This was seen, for example, in chess programs that went through possible games from the starting position and were now able to analyze move sequences further than before. Starting in the 1970s, chess AIs began to beat skilled human players, and finally, in 1997, IBM's Deep Blue supercomputer defeated the reigning world chess champion Garry Kasparov.

Despite the development of artificial intelligence, some problems still seemed extremely difficult to solve at the beginning of the 2000s. AI could beat humans at chess, but it was helpless in Go, where the number of possible move sequences grew much faster than in chess. In natural language problems, such as having a conversation with a human or automatic language translation, it seemed difficult to teach AI enough knowledge to understand context and the outside world.

---

[4] The Tower of Hanoi puzzle involves three pegs and a set of disks of different sizes. Initially, the disks are stacked in order on the left peg, with the largest at the bottom. The goal is to move the entire stack to the right peg, using the middle peg as an auxiliary. Only one disk may be moved at a time, and a larger disk may never be placed on top of a smaller one.

However, the situation changed suddenly with the development of machine learning methods and increased computing power. With neural networks and deep learning, impressive results have been achieved by training models with large datasets. In 2017, AlphaGo [11] defeated the world's best Go player. In the 2020s, large language models have made it possible to create AI applications that can perform tasks such as talking with people, generating code and translating languages.

References

1. J. Backus, R. Beeber, S. Best et al., *The Fortran Programmer's Reference Manual (Automatic Coding System for the IBM 704)*. IBM (1956)
2. J. Backus, The history of Fortran I, II, and III, in *History of Programming Languages* (ACM, 1978), 25–74
3. J.E. Sammet, The early history of COBOL, in *History of Programming Languages* (ACM, 1978), pp. 199–243
4. A.L. Tharp, The impact of fourth generation programming languages. ACM SIGCSE Bull. **16**(2), 37–44 (1984)
5. S.C. Johnson, Lint, a C Program Checker. (Bell Laboratories, 1978)
6. J.L. Bentley, M.D. McIlroy, Engineering a sort function. Softw.: Pract. Exp. **23**(11), 1249–1265 (1993)
7. A.M. Turing, Computing machinery and intelligence. Mind, LIX(236), 433–460 (1950)
8. C.E. Shannon, Programming a computer for playing chess. Philosoph. Mag. Ser. 7 **41**(314), 256–275 (1950)
9. J. McCarthy, History of LISP, in *History of Programming Languages* (ACM, 1978), pp. 173–185
10. J. Weizenbaum, ELIZA—a computer program for the study of natural language communication between man and machine. Commun. ACM **9**(1), 36–45 (1966)
11. D. Silver, J. Schrittwieser, K. Simonyan et al., Mastering the game of Go with deep neural networks and tree search. Nature **529**, 484–489 (2016)

Generative AI

3

This chapter provides an overview of how generative AI can be used in programming, as well as the benefits and risks of AI tools.

Section 3.1 explains how AI tools are used in software development to generate code. Both general-purpose chatbots and editor-integrated tools are based on large language models trained on extensive datasets.

Section 3.2 explores the field of prompt engineering, which focuses on creating prompts that yield useful results. We also discuss two characteristics of AI tools: nondeterminism, where identical prompts may produce different results, and hallucination, where outputs can be strange or misleading.

Section 3.3 outlines best practices for using AI tools in code generation and learning programming. The rise of AI tools does not remove the need for programmers' expertise. Instead, programmers should review AI-generated code and understand what the code does.

Section 3.4 examines the algorithms and concepts behind popular generative AI tools. Large language models are built on complex neural networks trained with large datasets and use advanced techniques to understand context and generate high-quality responses.

3.1 AI Tools in Programming

3.1.1 General-Purpose Chatbots

Chatbots, such as ChatGPT, have knowledge of programming and can generate, modify, and analyze code. Chatbots are used by writing *prompts* that can contain requests and questions. For example, let's use ChatGPT to generate code for finding the longest word in a list.

Prompt: I have a list that contains words. Create Python code that finds the longest word in the list.

Answer: Here is a simple Python code to find the longest word in a list:

```
words = ['apple', 'banana', 'watermelon', 'kiwi', 'grape']

# Find the longest word
longest_word = max(words, key=len)

print("The longest word is:", longest_word)
```

After that, we can continue the discussion and write another prompt that explains better what we would like to do:

Prompt: Actually, if the longest word is not unique, the code should choose the longest word that comes first in alphabetical order.

Answer: Great! Here's how you can find the first longest word in alphabetical order if there are ties:

```
words = ['apple', 'banana', 'watermelon', 'kiwi', 'grape',
         'pineapple', 'blackberry']

max_length = max(len(word) for word in words)
longest_words = [word for word in words if len(word) == max_length]
first_longest = min(longest_words)

print("The longest word is:", first_longest)
```

3.1.2 Editor-Integrated Tools

AI tools specialized in programming, such as GitHub Copilot, are typically integrated into programming editors and can be directly used while writing code. For example, suppose we have written the following code in Visual Studio Code with the GitHub Copilot plugin enabled:

```
words = ["monkey", "banana", "harpsichord"]

# Find the longest word
```

After writing the comment, Copilot suggests to add the following code:

```
longest_word = max(words, key=len)
```

We can accept the suggestion and complete the code by pressing the Tab key. After that, let's write another comment and the first line of the code:

3.1 AI Tools in Programming

```
# Find the first longest word in alphabetical order
word_lengths = [len(word) for word in words]
```

Again, Copilot automatically completes our code:

```
max_length = max(word_lengths)
candidates = [word for word in words if len(word) == max_length]
first_longest_word = min(candidates) if candidates else None
```

Code completion, as shown above, was one of the first features included in editor-integrated AI tools. Another common feature is explaining and analyzing code, which is similar to using a chatbot. Some tools can also perform more complex actions on the entire project consisting of several files, such as automatic refactoring, creating new files, and running terminal commands.

More advanced editor-integrated tools are sometimes called *AI agents*, which highlights their ability to work autonomously without the user having to request every step with a prompt. For example, the user can describe a required change to the project, and the AI agent will work on it independently, possibly for a long time, and then inform the user when it has finished its task.

3.1.3 Language Models

Generative AI tools are based on large language models that have been trained on large datasets. Different models are used in different AI tools, and there are often even several possible models available in a specific tool.

Some properties related to large language models are:

- *Architecture*: Neural networks are used to process input data and generate new content. The structure of the network and the number of parameters (such as the weights on the network's edges) affect the results produced by the network.
- *Training data*: During the training process, the parameters of the network are determined based on the training data. The training data typically includes content such as web pages and books.
- *Context size*: The maximum number of tokens[1] that the model can consider at the same time. The larger the context size, the more data from a prompt the model can remember and process.
- *Output size*: The maximum number of tokens that the model's output can contain. This limits the length of the answer the model can provide.
- *Knowledge cutoff*: A date after which events are not included in the language model's training data. The model cannot know what has happened after the knowledge cutoff.

---

[1] Large language models operate with *tokens*, which can be words, partial words, or characters. We discuss tokens further in Sect. 3.4.2.

Table 3.1 Features of OpenAI's language models

Model	Release date	Context size	Output size	Knowledge cutoff
GPT-5	August 2025	400,000	128,000	October 2024
GPT-4.1	April 2025	1,047,576	32,768	June 2024
GPT-4o	May 2024	128,000	16,384	October 2023

- *Costs*: The more computational power is needed to train the model and generate content with it, the more expensive it is.

Table 3.1 summarizes the features of OpenAI's recent language models.[2] For many new models, including those listed in the table, there is no published information about the detailed architecture of the model or the training data used. However, it was reported that the older GPT-3 model, released in 2020, has 175 billion parameters, and its training data included the Common Crawl web archive, collections of books, and Wikipedia data [1].

In general, newer language models are larger and produce better results, but there are also different types of models for different purposes. For example, some of OpenAI's newer models are *reasoning models* that can generate and improve answers in multiple steps. These models are specialized for solving problems that require complex reasoning.

3.1.4 Model Comparison

At the time of writing this book, there are no big differences in how popular language models generate code. As an example, here is a comparison in which we ask ChatGPT, Claude, DeepSeek, and Gemini to create a Python function that converts the given integer into a Roman numeral. For example, given the integer 143, the function should return "CXLIII". Here are the results:

ChatGPT

```python
def int_to_roman(num):
    val = [
        1000, 900, 500, 400, 100, 90, 50, 40, 10, 9, 5, 4, 1
    ]
    syb = [
        "M", "CM", "D", "CD", "C", "XC", "L", "XL", "X", "IX", "V", "IV",
        "I"
    ]
    roman_num = ''
    for i in range(len(val)):
        while num >= val[i]:
```

---

[2] https://platform.openai.com/docs/models/.

3.1 AI Tools in Programming

```
            roman_num += syb[i]
            num -= val[i]
    return roman_num
```

Claude

```
def int_to_roman(num):
    if not isinstance(num, int) or num <= 0 or num > 3999:
        raise ValueError("Input must be an integer between 1 and 3999")

    values = [1000, 900, 500, 400, 100, 90, 50, 40, 10, 9, 5, 4, 1]
    numerals = ["M", "CM", "D", "CD", "C", "XC", "L", "XL", "X", "IX", "V", "IV", "I"]

    result = ""

    for i in range(len(values)):
        count = num // values[i]
        if count:
            result += numerals[i] * count
            num -= values[i] * count

    return result
```

DeepSeek

```
def int_to_roman(num):
    if not isinstance(num, int) or num < 1 or num > 3999:
        raise ValueError("Input must be an integer between 1 and 3999")

    val_to_roman = [
        (1000, 'M'), (900, 'CM'), (500, 'D'), (400, 'CD'),
        (100, 'C'), (90, 'XC'), (50, 'L'), (40, 'XL'),
        (10, 'X'), (9, 'IX'), (5, 'V'), (4, 'IV'), (1, 'I')
    ]

    roman_num = []
    for val, sym in val_to_roman:
        while num >= val:
            roman_num.append(sym)
            num -= val
    return ''.join(roman_num)
```

Gemini

```
def int_to_roman(num: int) -> str:
    val = [
        1000, 900, 500, 400,
        100, 90, 50, 40,
        10, 9, 5, 4,
        1
    ]
    syb = [
        "M", "CM", "D", "CD",
        "C", "XC", "L", "XL",
        "X", "IX", "V", "IV",
        "I"
    ]
```

```
roman_numeral = ""
i = 0
while num > 0:
    for _ in range(num // val[i]):
        roman_numeral += syb[i]
        num -= val[i]
    i += 1
return roman_numeral
```

The general idea behind all of the above functions is the same: we process the letter combinations in order of decreasing value and add each combination to the result the correct number of times. For example, given the integer 143, we add "C" once, "XL" once and "I" three times to get the result "CXLIII".

All functions use descriptive names and good programming style. The name of the function is `int_to_roman` in all answers. However, there are small differences between the functions, such as:

- Claude and DeepSeek validate the input parameter, the others do not.
- Only Gemini includes type hints in the function signature.
- DeepSeek stores the letter combinations and their values as tuples, while the others use two separate lists.
- Claude repeats letter combinations using the * operator, Gemini uses a for loop and the others use a while loop.
- DeepSeek builds a result list and converts it to a string, while the others directly create the string.

Note that this comparison only shows the *default* programming style of the models in a single experiment at the time of writing this book. For example, while it appears that only Gemini includes type hints by default, we could ask the other models to include them as well by using a specific prompt.

3.1.5 Using Models Through APIs

Many language models can also be used programmatically via an API. We can define the prompt for the model in our code, and the response is automatically retrieved by sending a request to the model provider's server. Usually, using models through APIs requires authorization, and there is a cost for the tokens processed.

For example, OpenAI's language models can be used in Python as follows:[3]

---

[3] https://platform.openai.com/docs/quickstart.

3.2 Using Generative AI

```python
from openai import OpenAI

client = OpenAI()

response = client.responses.create(
    model="gpt-5",
    input="Write a brief history of the development of AI."
)

print(response.output_text)
```

In this book, we focus on using generative AI tools when programming, rather than calling language models through code. However, many of the topics discussed in the book about the possibilities and limitations of language models also apply to the latter situation.

3.2 Using Generative AI

3.2.1 Prompt Engineering

When traditional web search engines are used, the search query affects the quality of the results. Similarly, the prompt given to an AI tool influences the quality of its answer.

The skill of creating effective prompts is called *prompt engineering*. We can often improve the results of an AI tool by providing a more detailed description of what we want. For example, consider the following prompt, which asks for a JavaScript function that checks the contents of a grid:

Prompt: Create a JavaScript function that is given a two-dimensional square grid where each element is 0 or 1. The function should check if each column and row contains exactly one 1.

Answer: Below is a JavaScript function that checks if each row and column of a given two-dimensional square grid contains exactly one 1.

```javascript
function isValidGrid(grid) {
    const n = grid.length; // Get the size of the grid

    // Check each row
    for (let i = 0; i < n; i++) {
        let rowCount = 0;
        for (let j = 0; j < n; j++) {
            if (grid[i][j] === 1) {
                rowCount++;
            }
        }
        if (rowCount !== 1) {
            return false; // A row does not have exactly one 1
        }
    }

    // Check each column
```

```
        for (let j = 0; j < n; j++) {
            let colCount = 0;
            for (let i = 0; i < n; i++) {
                if (grid[i][j] === 1) {
                    colCount++;
                }
            }
            if (colCount !== 1) {
                return false; // A column does not have exactly one 1
            }
        }

        return true; // All rows and columns have exactly one 1
    }
```

The resulting function works, but from our programming experience, we know that it could be implemented in a better and more concise way. We also feel that comments are not necessary for such a simple function. To achieve a better result, we can extend the prompt and provide more information about our needs:

Prompt: Create a concise function and don't use comments.

Answer:

```
function isValidGrid(grid) {
    const n = grid.length;
    for (let i = 0; i < n; i++) {
        let rowCount = 0;
        let colCount = 0;
        for (let j = 0; j < n; j++) {
            rowCount += grid[i][j];
            colCount += grid[j][i];
        }
        if (rowCount !== 1 || colCount !== 1) return false;
    }
    return true;
}
```

3.2.2 Nondeterminism

Generative AI tools are usually *nondeterministic*, which means they include randomness when generating content. If we enter exactly the same prompt several times, we may get very different answers.

As an example, consider the task of creating a Python function that finds the most frequent element in a list. We can use the following prompt for this purpose:

Prompt: Create a Python function that finds the most frequent element in a list.

Answer: You can create a Python function to find the most frequent element in a list using the `collections.Counter` class, which makes it easy to count the occurrences of each element. Here's a simple implementation:

```python
from collections import Counter

def most_frequent_element(lst):
    if not lst:
        return None  # Return None if the list is empty
    
    # Create a Counter object to count the frequency of elements
    element_counts = Counter(lst)
    
    # Find the element with the highest frequency
    most_common_element, _ = element_counts.most_common(1)[0]
    
    return most_common_element
```

Now, let's start a new discussion and use exactly the same prompt again:

Prompt: Create a Python function that finds the most frequent element in a list.

Answer: Below is a Python function that finds the most frequent element in a list. If there are multiple elements with the same highest frequency, it returns the first one that appears in the list.

```python
def most_frequent_element(lst):
    if not lst:
        return None  # Return None if the list is empty
    
    frequency = {}
    
    # Count the frequency of each element
    for item in lst:
        if item in frequency:
            frequency[item] += 1
        else:
            frequency[item] = 1
    
    # Find the element with the highest frequency
    most_frequent = lst[0]
    max_count = frequency[most_frequent]
    
    for item, count in frequency.items():
        if count > max_count:
            most_frequent = item
            max_count = count
    
    return most_frequent
```

Now we have two different functions for finding the most frequent element in a list. The first function uses the `collections.Counter` class, while the second function uses a basic dictionary data structure. However, the functions also have some similarities: for example, they have the same function signature and handle the empty list in the same way.

If we use the above prompt repeatedly, it turns out that we do not get any new approaches to the problem. Each time, we receive a function that resembles either the first or the second function above. It seems that when we use the above prompt with a specific AI tool, there are essentially only two different approaches that the AI will suggest.

3.2.3 Hallucination

Like human beings, AI tools also make mistakes. It would be unrealistic to assume that using AI will always give us a perfect answer. However, a problem is that when AI tools provide incorrect information, they can be very convincing and try to please the user. The term *hallucination* is used to describe situations where AI tools give strange answers or make up things that do not exist.

For example, if a programmer believes that something exists, AI may try to please them by inventing what they are looking for. Consider the following prompt, which includes a correctly working C++ function for checking if a given word is a palindrome. The programmer suspects there is a bug in the function, and the AI "detects" a bug that does not actually exist.

Prompt: I have created the following C++ function to check if a word is a palindrome. However, it seems the function doesn't work correctly. Can you detect the bug in the code?

```cpp
bool is_palindrome(std::string word) {
    int n = word.size();
    for (int i = 0; i < n; i++) {
        if (word[i] != word[n - i - 1]) return false;
    }
    return true;
}
```

Answer: Yes, there is a bug in your `is_palindrome` function. The loop iterates from 0 to n, which means it will check the middle character twice when n is odd, and it will also access an out-of-bounds index when i becomes equal to n/2. To fix this, you should only iterate up to n/2, since you only need to compare the first half of the string with the second half. Here's the corrected code:

```cpp
bool is_palindrome(std::string word) {
    int n = word.size();
    for (int i = 0; i < n / 2; i++) { // Change to n / 2
        if (word[i] != word[n - i - 1]) return false;
    }
    return true;
}
```

With this change, the function will correctly check for palindromes by comparing the characters only up to the middle of the string, avoiding any out-of-bounds access.

The answer given by the AI claims that the bug in the function is that the loop will access an out-of-bounds index. This is not true: since i is always between 0 and $n-1$, the value of $n-i-1$ is also between 0 and $n-1$, so the code does not access an out-of-bounds index. Note that the "corrected" code also works correctly because it is enough to check the indices between 0 and $\lfloor n/2 \rfloor - 1$, but such a change is not needed to fix any bug in the code.

Let's consider another example where we ask for an efficient algorithm for a problem. Our task is to divide the numbers $1, 2, \ldots, n$ into three sets so that the sum of numbers in each set is the same. For example, when $n = 5$, we can create the sets $\{1, 4\}$, $\{2, 3\}$, and $\{5\}$. This solution is valid because the sum of each set is 5. Creating the sets is not always possible. For example, when $n = 4$, the sum $1+2+3+4 = 10$ is not divisible by 3 and there is no solution.

Prompt: Create an efficient Python solution for the following problem. You are given an integer n and your task is to divide the numbers $1, 2, \ldots, n$ into three sets so that the sum of numbers in each set is the same. You should also detect if there is no solution.

Answer: For the numbers 1 to n to be divided into three sets with equal sums, the total sum $n(n+1)/2$ must be divisible by 3. If possible, we iteratively assign the largest available number to the set with the current smallest sum, ensuring all sets reach the target sum.

```
def divide_into_three_sets(n):
    S = n * (n + 1) // 2
    if S % 3 != 0:
        return None  # Not possible
    target = S // 3
    sets = [[], [], []]
    sums = [0, 0, 0]
    for num in range(n, 0, -1):
        idx = sums.index(min(sums))
        sets[idx].append(num)
        sums[idx] += num
    if all(s == target for s in sums):
        return sets
    return None
```

Does the algorithm work? For example, when $n = 5$, the algorithm creates the sets $\{1, 4\}$, $\{2, 3\}$, and $\{5\}$, which looks good. The algorithm works in many cases, which makes the answer convincing, because we can test the algorithm with several examples and see that it produces correct results. However, there are cases where the algorithm does not work. One such case is $n = 8$: the algorithm reports that there is no solution, but it is actually possible to create the sets $\{1, 2, 3, 6\}$, $\{4, 8\}$, and $\{5, 7\}$. Thus, the approach suggested by the AI is not correct.

Because of hallucination, we must be suspicious of any answer given by generative AI. One specific threat in software development is package hallucination [2], also called *slopsquatting*. In this, a malicious person notices that AI often suggests using a certain package that does not exist. The person can then create a package with this name containing harmful code and get people to use it because AI recommends the package.

3.3 Best Practices for Using AI

3.3.1 Code Generation

A good rule of thumb is: before using AI-generated code, a human must check and understand the code. Using unknown code without reviewing would be risky. In fact, in a professional software project, even when a human programmer wants to add new code, someone else should review it.

A safe way to use AI is to generate code that you, as a programmer, *could* write yourself by traditional means, but you use AI to create the code more efficiently. When you already have a general idea of what the resulting code should look like, it helps you check the generated code. For example, consider the task of creating JavaScript code that displays a grid in a canvas element:

Prompt: Create JavaScript code that shows a 10x10 grid in a canvas element.

Answer: Here's a JavaScript code snippet that creates a 10x10 grid in a `<canvas>` element:

```
<canvas id="gridCanvas" width="400" height="400"></canvas>
<script>
    const canvas = document.getElementById('gridCanvas');
    const ctx = canvas.getContext('2d');
    const size = 40; // Size of each cell

    for (let i = 0; i <= 10; i++) {
        ctx.moveTo(i * size, 0);
        ctx.lineTo(i * size, 400);
        ctx.moveTo(0, i * size);
        ctx.lineTo(400, i * size);
    }
    ctx.stroke();
</script>
```

The code above contains many details that can be difficult to *remember* if you don't write JavaScript code and use canvas elements often, such as how to define the drawing context (`getContext`) and what methods can be used to draw lines (`moveTo`, `lineTo` and `stroke`). However, when you see the generated code, it can be easy to *check* that it does reasonable things.

A more difficult situation arises when you use AI tools for a task that is unfamiliar to you. In this case, checking the code can be much harder because you would first need to learn about the topic. For example, suppose we generate the following code without having a background in statistics or machine learning:

3.3 Best Practices for Using AI

Prompt: I have some data on how many items of a product are sold in different months in different shops. Can you create code that can be used to predict the number of items sold, given the place and month?

Answer: You can use a machine learning approach to predict the number of items sold based on the shop and month. One common way to do this is to use a regression model. Below is an example code using Python with the `pandas` and `scikit-learn` libraries.

```
import pandas as pd
from sklearn.model_selection import train_test_split
from sklearn.linear_model import LinearRegression
from sklearn.preprocessing import OneHotEncoder
from sklearn.compose import ColumnTransformer
from sklearn.pipeline import Pipeline

# Load the data
data = pd.read_csv('your_data.csv')

# Split the data into features and target variable
X = data[['shop', 'month']]
y = data['items_sold']

# Create a pipeline that preprocesses the data and fits a linear
    regression model
model = Pipeline(steps=[
    ('preprocessor', ColumnTransformer(transformers=[('cat',
    OneHotEncoder(), ['shop', 'month'])])),
    ('regressor', LinearRegression())
])

# Train the model
model.fit(*train_test_split(X, y, test_size=0.2, random_state=42))

# Function to predict items sold
def predict_items_sold(shop, month):
    return model.predict(pd.DataFrame({'shop': [shop], 'month': [
        month]}))[0]

# Example usage
print(f'Predicted items sold in Shop A in January: {
    predict_items_sold("Shop A", "January")}')
```

Even if the prompt was vague, the AI still produced a piece of code that we could use directly. The generated code may or may not work, but before using it, we should understand several things, such as:

- What are the `pandas` and `scikit-learn` libraries? Are they good libraries in this situation?
- What is the data format of the CSV file?
- What are features and target variables?
- What are pipelines, transformers and encoders?
- Is the linear regression model a good model here?
- What other possible models are there? How do we actually know which model we should use?
- What do test size 0.2 and random state 42 mean?
- How do we know if the predictions are good?

In this situation, to produce professional code, we should first familiarize ourselves with the different models and libraries that could be used. Only after that do we know what we want to do and are able to evaluate AI-generated code.

3.3.2 Learning Programming

AI tools can be used in many ways when learning programming and related skills. However, while they can provide good answers to many questions, there is a potential danger when using them: we may not learn what we should learn, and even worse, we may still think that we are learning well.

As an example, assume a beginner programmer is learning the basics of Python programming and cannot solve an exercise given in the course. In this situation, they can conveniently use AI as follows:

Prompt: I'm learning the basics of Python programming. I need to create a function that is given a parameter n. The function should return a list $[1, n, 2, n - 1, ...]$. For example, the result for $n = 7$ should be $[1, 7, 2, 6, 3, 5, 4]$. I can't solve the problem. Can you show how to create the function and explain the code?

Answer: Let's create a function that generates the desired list based on the input parameter n. The pattern you want to achieve is to alternate between counting up from 1 and counting down from n.

Here's how you can implement this in Python:

```python
def create_list(n):
    result = []
    for i in range(1, (n // 2) + 1):
        result.append(i)           # Append the counting up number
        result.append(n - i + 1)   # Append the counting down number
    if n % 2 == 1:                 # If n is odd, add the middle number
        result.append((n // 2) + 1)
    return result
```

Explanation of the Code:
- Function Definition: We define a function named `create_list` that takes one parameter n.
- Initialization of Result List: We initialize an empty list called `result` that will hold the final output.
- Looping: We use a `for` loop that iterates from 1 to $\frac{n}{2}$ (inclusive).

  – The expression (n // 2) + 1 ensures that if n is even, we go up to $\frac{n}{2}$ and if n is odd, we still include the middle number later.

- Appending Elements:

  – Inside the loop, we first append the current value of i (which counts up from 1).
  – We then append the corresponding value from the end of the range, which is calculated as $n - i + 1$. This formula gives us the numbers counting down from n.

- Handling Odd n: After the loop, we check if n is odd using `if n % 2 == 1`. If it is, we append the middle number, which is $\frac{n}{2} + 1$.
- Return the Result: Finally, we return the `result` list.

In this case, AI provided a good solution to the problem, along with a detailed explanation. In fact, it would be possible to solve almost every problem in a typical programming course using the same method, learning by reading code and explanations. If something in the code is unclear, we could ask follow-up questions and use AI as our personal tutor as much as we want. However, although we can do this, it would be a big mistake to learn programming in this way.

The problem is that the real purpose of exercises like the one above is not to teach information retrieval. The goal is not to learn techniques for automatically generating answers to programming problems: it is not a great achievement to enter the problem statement into an AI tool and copy-paste the answer. Instead, the goal is to learn how to solve such problems *independently*. We should learn what programming is about and how to think and design programs.

Writing new code from scratch and reading existing code are two very different things. Even if you can understand code written by someone else (or think that you understand it), this does not guarantee that you could create any new code by yourself. Similarly, you can easily read a famous novel and *understand* every sentence in the book, but it would be a very different and much more difficult task to *write* a new book like that.

3.4 Inside AI Tools

3.4.1 Language Models

Generative AI tools are based on *language models* that can generate content by following rules learned from *training data*. Here, *language* can refer to a natural language like English, a programming language like Python, or any other system that consists of sequences of symbols.

For example, consider the task of generating English text using a language model. Typically, the input to the model is a sequence of words, and the model should predict the next word. For instance, given the input "Python is a programming", the model might choose "language" as the next word.

Once we have a working language model that can predict the next word, we can repeatedly use the model to generate text word by word. For example, we could generate a full sentence as follows:

1. Input: "Python"
   Output: "is"
2. Input: "Python is"
   Output: "a"

Fig. 3.1 Part of a Markov model that contains three possible words after "programming" with different probabilities

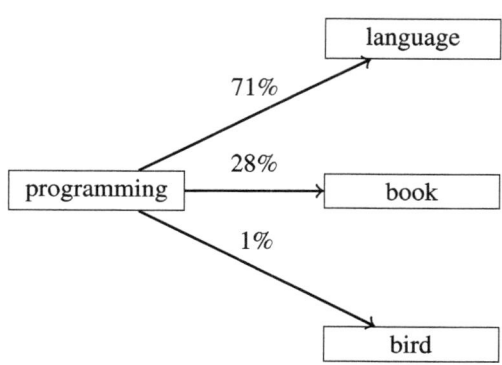

3. Input: "Python is a"
   Output: "programming"
4. Input: "Python is a programming"
   Output: "language"

Here the initial input for the model was "Python", and after four steps, we generated the sentence "Python is a programming language".

Using the same principle, we could use a language model to generate Python code. For example, if we have the tokens `for name in` as the input, the model could predict that the next token is `names`, which results in a Python for loop that iterates through a list of names.

The challenge is how to create a language model that can make good predictions and generate meaningful content. Consider again the situation where we want to generate text in English. One simple way to do this is to go through a large amount of text written in English and, for each word, create a list of words that often follow it. For example, the word that comes after "programming" is often "language" and rarely "bird". Thus, if we know that the current word is "programming", it is better to predict that the next word will be "language" rather than "bird".

The approach described above is used in *Markov models*, which can be represented as graphs whose nodes are words and whose edges are connections with probabilities. Figure 3.1 shows part of a Markov model that contains nodes for four words: "programming", "language", "book", and "bird". The next word after "programming" is "language" with probability 71%, "book" with probability 28%, and "bird" with probability 1%. Thus, if the current word is "programming", the model usually predicts "language" or "book" as the next word.

The problem with Markov models is that their context is very limited. In the model described above, only the last word in the current sequence is considered when choosing the next word. This is usually not enough. For example, the next word after "Python is a programming" should be "language", but the next word after "I read a programming" should be "book". If we only consider the last word, "programming", it is impossible to know which choice to make.

To generate meaningful results, a language model should be able to consider a larger number of previous words when choosing the next word and understand the role of different word combinations. Developing such a model is much more difficult than creating a simple Markov model. Next, we will explore some ideas used in *generative pretrained transformers* (GPTs), which are used in popular large language models, such as the ones used in ChatGPT.

3.4.2 Tokens and Embeddings

In practice, a language model that works with a dictionary of English words or any other fixed set of words would be quite limited. For example, consider the input "I know a man called Uolevi". The name Uolevi does not appear in many word lists, yet the language model should still be able to suggest the next word after it.

In real-world language models, *tokens* are used instead of words. A token is a string that can be a word, part of a word, or a single character. The input string is represented as a sequence of tokens, and the language model predicts the next token. This makes the model flexible, allowing it to handle arbitrary words and other character sequences.

The set of tokens depends on the language model used. The OpenAI platform includes a tool called *Tokenizer*[4], which represents a given string as a sequence of tokens. For example, the token sequence for the string "I know a man called Uolevi" can be as follows:

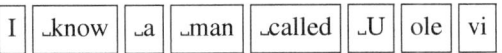

Here, the symbol "␣" represents a space, and most tokens are English words that are preceded by spaces. However, the name Uolevi, which is not a common word, is made up of three tokens: "␣U", "ole", and "vi". With this approach, common words can be conveniently represented as single tokens, while less common words, such as the name Uolevi, can be formed by combining smaller tokens.

As another example, consider the following Python code:

```
def count_words(text):
    return len(text.split(" "))
```

This code can be represented using 12 tokens as follows:

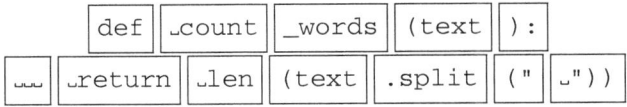

---

[4] https://platform.openai.com/tokenizer.

Besides tokens, *embeddings* are used in language models. An embedding is a list of numbers that represents some piece of information, such as a token, a word or a sentence. An embedding might look like this:

$$[0.05956292, 0.51449084, 0.21927416, 0.30079162, \dots]$$

Embeddings may look like random lists of numbers, but their purpose is to capture useful information that can be used when processing data. For example, if two words are similar (such as "big" and "large"), their embeddings should also be similar. Embeddings are helpful in language models because neural networks work with numbers and can learn relationships through embeddings.

3.4.3 Neural Networks

Large language models are based on *neural networks* with deep and complex structures. Still, the basic idea behind these models is the same as what we discussed earlier with simple models. The network receives a sequence of tokens as input, uses embeddings to process the data, and finally outputs a probability distribution that gives, for each possible token, the probability of being the next token in the sequence (Fig. 3.2).

The *parameters* of the network, such as the weights on its edges, determine how the network processes data. These parameters are learned during the training process. Since the task of the network is to predict the next token in a sequence, it can be trained using token sequences from the training data. For example, suppose the training data contains the sentence "Python is a programming language". In this case, the network is considered to perform well if it produces the output "language" when given the input "Python is a programming". During training, the parameters are adjusted so that the network generates content similar to the training data.

Interestingly, while large language models are observed to provide good results, it is very difficult to understand what really happens inside their neural networks. After training, the network parameters are random-looking numbers that often do not have any clear interpretation. However, the idea is that the parameters store information

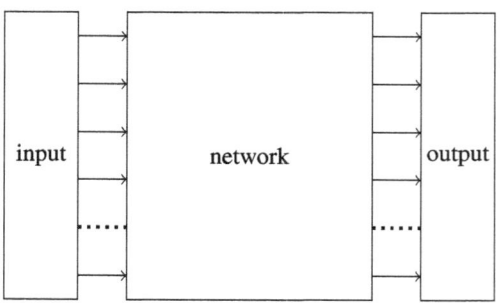

Fig. 3.2 The overall structure of a large language model. The input is a sequence of tokens, and the output is a probability distribution for the next token

learned from the training data, and the network can generalize this information to process inputs that were not directly included in the training data.

Knowing the overall neural network structure used in large language models can help us understand some of their properties and limitations. First, there is randomness in AI tools because the output of the neural network is a probability distribution, and there may be several suitable choices for the next token. Hallucination can be explained by the fact that the parameters of the network approximate the patterns found in the training material, and the AI has been trained to predict the next token in the sequence even if there is not enough data to predict it reliably. There are token limits in AI input and output because the network size is limited.

3.4.4 Context and Attention

To produce high-quality results, the language model should consider the context of the tokens in the input sequence. For example, consider the input sequence "Python was released in". In this case, the next word should be a year, and more specifically, the year when the Python programming language was released.

Here is some reasoning that could be useful in this situation:

- The word "Python" refers to a programming language, not to an animal or something else. The word "released" suggests that "Python" is a programming language in this context.
- There should be a year after the word "in", not a place or something else. The words "Python" and "released" suggest this because it is common to mention the year when a programming language was released.
- The year should be the year the Python programming language was released. The word "Python" suggests this.
- There is no version number given, so we should probably give the year when the first version of Python was released.

Similarly, to generate and analyze code, the language model should consider the context. For example, assume that the input sequence contains the following code:

```
import random
n = 100
numbers = list(range(n))

# Shuffle the list
```

To generate the next code line, there should be some reasoning such as:

- The programming language used is Python, based on the code provided so far.
- The `random` module has already been imported, so it can be used to shuffle the list.

- There is a list called `numbers`; this is probably the list that should be shuffled.
- The variable `n` is not important here, we should not focus on it.

It has turned out that the attention mechanism [3] is an effective way to include this kind of reasoning in neural networks. The high-level idea is to compare input tokens and learn which tokens are relevant for predicting the next token, and how they affect the prediction. For example, to understand the context of the word "Python" in our previous example, the network could intuitively scan the other words in the input, find the word "released", and conclude that the combination of "Python" and "released" means that "Python" is probably a programming language.

3.4.5 Fine-Tuning and Prompting

Even if a language model has learned to produce text that closely resembles its training data, the model still cannot be used as is in many applications. For example, chatbots should interact with users in a friendly manner, but anyone who has used the internet knows that online discussion is not always friendly. For example, when a user asks a simple programming-related question, the chatbot should never answer with a link to the "Let Me Google That" website[5], even if there would be such answers in the training data.

To make language models work better in real-world applications, they are *fine-tuned* after the main training process. This can include people showing examples of how the AI should respond and evaluating different answers given by the AI. With this approach, it is possible to influence the tone the AI uses when talking to users, how long its answers are, and also the style in which the AI writes code.

The way AI tools work can also be changed by using prompts with instructions about how the AI should behave during the conversation. A *system prompt* is given to the AI before it starts a conversation with a human. For example, the general system prompt used with the Claude Opus 4 model (version from May 22, 2025) includes the following instructions related to malicious code:[6]

> Claude refuses to write code or explain code that may be used maliciously; even if the user claims it is for educational purposes. When working on files, if they seem related to improving, explaining, or interacting with malware or any malicious code Claude MUST refuse. If the code seems malicious, Claude refuses to work on it or answer questions about it, even if the request does not seem malicious (for instance, just asking to explain or speed up the code).

---

[5] Some people use "Let Me Google That" (https://letmegooglethat.com/) when a beginner asks a question that could easily be answered with a quick Google search. The website shows an animation where the question is typed into Google's search box, and the mouse clicks the button to perform the search.

[6] https://docs.anthropic.com/en/release-notes/system-prompts.

References

1. T.B. Brown, B. Mann, N. Ryder et al. Language models are few-shot learners. Adv. Neural Inf. Proc. Syst. (2020)
2. J. Spracklen, R. Wijewickrama, A.H.M.N. Sakib, et al. We have a package for you! A comprehensive analysis of package hallucinations by code generating LLMs (2025). arXiv:2406.10279
3. A. Vaswani, N. Shazeer, N. Parmar, et al. Attention is all you need. Advances in Neural Information Processing Systems (2017)

Information Retrieval

4

This chapter discusses the use of generative AI for retrieving programming-related information. AI tools can be considered an alternative to web search engines for finding information. Getting answers by writing prompts can be easier and faster than using traditional search engines.

Section 4.1 compares answers generated by AI tools with those found using a web search engine. AI tools can be a more convenient alternative because they can give relevant answers right away, without the need to browse through websites.

Section 4.2 looks at a more advanced way to use AI tools for information retrieval by including more context, such as a piece of code in our prompt. This is helpful when we are looking for information about a programming concept or situation that is hard to describe with words.

Section 4.3 focuses on collecting information from several sources and creating summaries. This is useful, for example, when we need a library for a specific programming task and want to compare different solutions.

Section 4.4 discusses the accuracy of AI-generated content. While we should check answers generated by AI-tools, the same applies to answers from people and websites. However, incorrect AI-generated answers can seem more convincing than those found through traditional means.

4.1 AI Versus Search Engines

Generative AI tools and traditional web search engineshave several things in common. Both rely on large amounts of data, and both training AI models and creating search indexes take time. AI tools aim to generate relevant answers to prompts, while search engines try to find relevant pages related to search queries.

Finding relevant information using web search engines can be difficult and may require browsing through many websites. Generative AI tools can help with this because they try to provide a direct and useful answer to a question. In this section, we compare the results of ChatGPT and Google in programming-related information retrieval tasks.

4.1.1 String Reversal Function

As the first example, consider the task of reversing a string in JavaScript. For example, given the string `hello`, the result should be `olleh`. Let's first use ChatGPT for solving the task:

> *Prompt*: How can I reverse a string in JavaScript?
>
> *Answer*: To reverse a string in JavaScript, you can follow these steps:
>
> 1. Convert the string into an array of characters.
> 2. Reverse the array.
> 3. Join the array back into a string.
>   Here's a simple function that demonstrates this process:
>
> ```
> function reverseString(str) {
>     return str.split('').reverse().join('');
> }
>
> // Example usage:
> const originalString = "Hello, World!";
> const reversedString = reverseString(originalString);
> console.log(reversedString); // Output: "!dlroW ,olleH"
> ```

This is a good answer and the usual way to reverse a string in JavaScript.

Then, what happens when we try to solve the problem by doing a Google search? The first result for the query "reverse string javascript" is an article published at freeCodeCamp with the title *Three Ways to Reverse a String in JavaScript*.[1] The article begins with the following introduction:

> Reversing a string is one of the most frequently asked JavaScript question in the technical round of interview. Interviewers may ask you to write different ways to reverse a string, or they may ask you to reverse a string without using in-built methods, or they may even ask you to reverse a string using recursion.

After scrolling down the page for a while, we find the first suggested method for reversing a string, which is almost identical to the AI-generated code:

---

[1] https://www.freecodecamp.org/news/75e4763c68cb.

4.1 AI Versus Search Engines

```
function reverseString(str) {
    return str.split("").reverse().join("");
}
reverseString("hello");
```

In this case, we found the same method for reversing a string using both ChatGPT and Google. However, using ChatGPT was more convenient: we got the information we wanted right away, without having to browse through search results and scroll the page to find the relevant details.

On the other hand, with Google, we know the source of our information. We can see the author of the article and the publication date (March 2016). Since the article was published a long time ago, we might wonder if there is a more modern way to reverse strings in JavaScript. We could also look through more search results to find additional information.

4.1.2 Random Integer Generation

Next, let's find information about generating random integers in C++. More specifically, we want to generate a random integer between 1 and 100. We get the following answer using ChatGPT:

Prompt: How can I generate a random integer between 1 and 100 using C++?

Answer: To generate a random integer between 1 and 100 in C++, you can use the `<random>` library, which provides a modern and flexible way to generate random numbers. Here's a simple example of how to do this:

```cpp
#include <iostream>
#include <random>

int main() {
    // Create a random device and a random number generator
    std::random_device rd;   // Obtain a random number from hardware
    std::mt19937 eng(rd());  // Seed the generator

    // Define the range [1, 100]
    std::uniform_int_distribution<> distr(1, 100);

    // Generate and print a random number
    int random_number = distr(eng);
    std::cout << "Random number between 1 and 100: " <<
      random_number << std::endl;
}
```

Then, the Google search "c++ random integer between 1 and 100" leads us to a Stack Overflow question with the title *How do I generate random numbers in a range?*[2] in the C++ section. The first answer to the question is as follows:

> To generate a random number in C++11 or later, use the C++ random library. This should be much preferred over the C utilities for any application.
>
> ```
> #include <random>
> #include <iostream>
>
> int main() {
>   std::random_device seed;
>   std::mt19937 gen{seed()}; // seed the generator
>   std::uniform_int_distribution<> dist{47, 89}; // set min and max
>   int guess = dist(gen); // generate number
>   std::cout << "Computer guess: " << guess << '\n';
> }
> ```
>
> Read the relevant cppreference page for more information.

Again, both answers are almost identical. The only difference is that the AI-generated code generates an integer between 1 and 100, as we asked, while the Stack Overflow example generates an integer between 47 and 89, so we would need to change it a bit. Also, the Stack Overflow answer includes a link to a C++ reference, which has more information on the topic.

It is worth noting that the Stack Overflow page shown as the first search result does not discuss the range from 1 to 100, yet Google still chose it as the most relevant result. Modern search engines do not just compare strings directly; they also use more advanced techniques (including AI) to find answers that match the query.

4.1.3 Function Syntax Reference

In the following example, we want to know the syntax of the `explode` function in PHP. This function creates an array from a string using a delimiter. As before, we first use ChatGPT to find the information:

> *Prompt*: What is the syntax of the `explode` function in PHP?
>
> *Answer*: The `explode` function in PHP is used to split a string into an array based on a specified delimiter. The syntax of the `explode` function is as follows:
>
> ```
> array explode(string $delimiter, string $string[, int $limit =
>     PHP_INT_MAX])
> ```

---

[2] https://stackoverflow.com/q/55786909.

4.1 AI Versus Search Engines

> Parameters
> - $delimiter: The boundary string at which to split the input string. This parameter is required.
> - $string: The input string to be split. This parameter is also required.
> - $limit (optional): If specified, this parameter limits the number of elements in the resulting array. The default value is PHP_INT_MAX, which means there is no limit on the number of elements. If the limit is positive, the returned array will contain at most limit elements, and the last element will contain the rest of the string. If the limit is negative, all components except for the last |limit| elements will be returned.
>
> Return Value
>
> The explode function returns an array of strings created by splitting the input string at each occurrence of the delimiter. If the delimiter is not found in the string, it returns an array containing the original string as its only element.
>
> [...]

Using Google, the first search result takes us to the official PHP documentation which has a page that describes the explode function:

> Description
>
> > **explode**(string $separator, string $string, int $limit = PHP_INT_MAX) : **array**
>
> Returns an array of strings, each of which is a substring of string formed by splitting it on boundaries formed by the string separator.
>
> Parameters
> - separator: The boundary string.
> - string: The input string.
> - limit: If limit is set and positive, the returned array will contain a maximum of limit elements with the last element containing the rest of string.
>
> If the limit parameter is negative, all components except the last -limit are returned.
>
> If the limit parameter is zero, then this is treated as 1.
>
> Note: Prior to PHP 8.0, implode() accepted its parameters in either order. explode() has never supported this: you must ensure that the separator argument comes before the string argument.
>
> Return Values
>
> Returns an array of strings created by splitting the string parameter on boundaries formed by the separator.
>
> If separator is an empty string (""), explode() throws a ValueError. If separator contains a value that is not contained in string and a negative limit is used, then an empty array will be returned, otherwise an array containing string will be returned. If separator values appear at the start or end of string, said values will be added as an empty array value either in the first or last position of the returned array respectively.
>
> [...]

Also in this example, the AI-generated answer and the PHP documentation page are quite similar. However, the PHP documentation page contains more information: it explains what happens when the limit parameter is zero and discusses more special cases in the return values. In most cases, though, the AI-generated answer is probably comprehensive enough.

4.2 Adding Context to Search

When using traditional search engines, it can be difficult to create good search queries because some programming concepts and situations are hard to describe in just a few words. In such cases, AI tools can be helpful because we can give them more context, such as a piece of code.

4.2.1 Search by Example

Suppose we are interested in *operator precedence*, which means that if we have an expression `a and b or c`, the part `a and b` is evaluated first. In other words, the expressions `a and b or c` and `(a and b) or c` are equal.

If we already know the name of this concept, it is easy to use the query "operator precedence" to find information with web search engines. However, if we don't know the term beforehand, it is more difficult to create a good query. With AI tools, we can simply show example code in the prompt:

Prompt: If you have code like this:

```
if a and b or c:
    ...
```

This equals the following code:

```
if (a and b) or c:
    ...
```

What is the name of this phenomenon and what are the exact rules?

Answer: The phenomenon you are describing is related to the concept of operator precedence in programming languages, particularly in Python.
Operator precedence determines the order in which different operators are evaluated in an expression. In Python, the logical operators have the following precedence (from highest to lowest): 1. `not`, 2. `and`, 3. `or`.
In your example:

```
if a and b or c:
```

The `and` operator has a higher precedence than the `or` operator. Therefore, the expression is evaluated as:

```
if (a and b) or c:
```

This means that `a and b` is evaluated first, and then the result of that evaluation is combined with `c` using the `or` operator.

4.2.2 Interpreting Error Messages

AI tools are good at providing targeted help for interpreting error messages in programming. Unlike traditional search engines, we can include our code to provide more context.

In the following example, our Python code produces a syntax error message. Searching the internet for information using such a generic error message could be difficult, but the problem can be easily solved with AI.

Prompt: I try to use the following Python function in my code:

```python
def get_direction(symbol):
    match symbol:
        case "L":
            return "left"
        case "R":
            return "right"
```

However, I get the following error message:

```
  File "test.py", line 2
    match symbol:
        ^
SyntaxError: invalid syntax
```

How can I fix the error?

Answer: The `match` statement was introduced in Python 3.10. If you are using an earlier version, you'll get a `SyntaxError`. To fix the error, either upgrade your Python to 3.10 or later, or replace the `match` statement with a standard `if-elif` block:

```python
def get_direction(symbol):
    if symbol == "L":
        return "left"
    elif symbol == "R":
        return "right"
```

4.3 Collecting Information

Another benefit of using AI tools for information retrieval is that they can gather information from multiple sources and create summaries. While we could usually find the same information with traditional search engines, it might require browsing through a large number of websites.

4.3.1 Deprecated HTML Tags

As the first example, suppose we need a list of HTML tags that are now *deprecated*, i.e., it is not recommended to use them anymore and modern browsers may not support them. Let's create such a list:

Prompt: Create a list of all HTML tags that have been deprecated. For each tag, briefly describe how it was used and why it is now deprecated.
Use the following format for each list entry:
[tag name]: [description]

Answer: Here is a list of HTML tags that have been deprecated, along with their usage and reasons for deprecation:
 `<acronym>`: Used to mark up acronyms. Deprecated in favor of `<abbr>`, as both serve similar purposes and `<abbr>` is preferred for all abbreviations.
 `<applet>`: Used to embed Java applets. Deprecated because of security issues and the decline of Java applets; replaced by `<object>`.
 `<basefont>`: Used to set a default font size, color, and face for the document. Deprecated in favor of CSS for styling.
 `<big>`: Used to make text larger. Deprecated; use CSS (e.g., `font-size`) instead.
 `<blink>`: Used to make text blink (non-standard, but supported in some browsers). Deprecated due to poor usability and lack of support.
 `<center>`: Used to center-align text or content. Deprecated in favor of CSS.
 `<dir>`: Used to create a directory list. Deprecated; use `<ul>` for unordered lists.
 `<font>`: Used to specify font face, size, and color. Deprecated in favor of CSS for all font styling.
 `<frame>`: Used to define a particular frame in a `<frameset>`. Deprecated due to usability and accessibility issues; use `<iframe>` for inline frames.
 `<frameset>`: Used to define a set of frames. Deprecated; replaced by CSS layouts and `<iframe>`.
 `<isindex>`: Used to provide a single-line text input for searching. Deprecated; use `<form>` with `<input>` elements instead.
 `<listing>`: Used to display preformatted text. Deprecated; use `<pre>` instead.
 `<marquee>`: Used to create scrolling text or images. Deprecated due to poor usability and lack of standardization; use CSS animations instead.
 `<menu>` (in HTML4): Used for single-column menu lists. Deprecated; `<ul>` is used for lists. (Note: `<menu>` was reintroduced in HTML5 with a different purpose.)
 `<multicol>`: Used to create multi-column text. Deprecated; use CSS multi-column layouts.
 `<nobr>`: Used to prevent text from wrapping. Deprecated; use CSS `white-space: nowrap` instead.
 `<noembed>`: Used as fallback content for browsers that do not support `<embed>`. Deprecated; use `<object>` with fallback content.
 `<noframes>`: Used to provide alternate content for browsers that do not support frames. Deprecated along with `<frameset>`.
 `<plaintext>`: Used to render everything that follows as plain text. Deprecated; use `<pre>` for preformatted text.
 `<s>`: Used to render strikethrough text. Deprecated in HTML4 in favor of `<del>` or `<strike>`, but reintroduced in HTML5 for specific cases.
 `<spacer>`: Used to create space between elements. Deprecated; use CSS `margin` or `padding`.
 `<strike>`: Used to render strikethrough text. Deprecated; use `<del>` or `<s>` instead.
 `<tt>`: Used to render text in teletype or monospace font. Deprecated in favor of CSS.
 `<u>`: Used to underline text. Deprecated in HTML4 in favor of CSS, but reintroduced in HTML5 for non-textual annotation.
 `<xmp>`: Used to display preformatted text and escape HTML. Deprecated; use `<pre>` and `<code>` instead.

Generating the above list using AI was definitely easier than using a traditional search engine. On the other hand, there are some potential issues we should keep in mind. First, we do not know if the list is complete or if all the facts are correct. In particular, it is hard for us to know if any tag is missing. Second, we did not clearly define what a deprecated tag means. Do we only consider tags that have appeared in web standards, or also browser-specific tags?[3]

4.3.2 Handling Big Integers

As another example, suppose we need a library for handling big integers in C. To compare the syntax used in different libraries, we also request a code example for each library that shows how to calculate the factorial of 100 using that library.

Prompt: I need a library for handling big integers in C. Can you show me the best libraries for that? For each library, show how the factorial of 100 can be calculated.

Answer: Here are some of the best libraries for big integers in C, along with example code for calculating the factorial of 100.
    1. GMP (GNU Multiple Precision Arithmetic Library): A widely-used, high-performance library for arbitrary-precision arithmetic, supporting integers, rational numbers, and floating-point numbers.

```
mpz_t fact;
mpz_init_set_ui(fact, 1);

for (int i = 2; i <= 100; ++i) {
    mpz_mul_ui(fact, fact, i);
}

gmp_printf("%Zd\n", fact);
mpz_clear(fact);
```

    2. LibTomMath: A lightweight, portable, and easy-to-integrate multiple-precision integer library, suitable for embedded systems and cryptography.

```
mp_int fact;
mp_init(&fact);
mp_set_int(&fact, 1);

for (int i = 2; i <= 100; ++i) {
    mp_mul_d(&fact, i, &fact);
}

char *str = mp_to_decimal(&fact);
printf("%s\n", str);
mp_free(str);
mp_clear(&fact);
```

---

[3] For example, the list does not include the <bgsound> tag which could be used in Internet Explorer to play background music.

3. FLINT (Fast Library for Number Theory): A high-performance C library for number theory applications, supporting fast arbitrary-precision integer arithmetic.

```
fmpz_t fact;
fmpz_init_set_ui(fact, 1);

for (int i = 2; i <= 100; ++i) {
    fmpz_mul_ui(fact, fact, i);
}

fmpz_print(fact);
printf("\n");
fmpz_clear(fact);
```

Here, it is useful that we can automatically generate code for the same example task using each library, which makes it easier to compare their syntaxes. However, we do not know much about the libraries based on the answer above, for example, how efficient they are in specific use cases. To learn more, it would be good to test each library in practice before deciding which one to use.

4.4 AI Content Accuracy

How can we know if AI-generated content is accurate? We cannot know for sure before verifying it. In fact, this is not something we should do only for AI-generated content. If we find some information on the internet, we should not assume it is true before checking it. Similarly, if a colleague or friend tells us something, we should verify it before believing it.

Often there are two simple things we can do: read through the generated code and test it by running it. For example, consider the following AI-generated JavaScript function for reversing a string:

```
function reverseString(str) {
    return str.split('').reverse().join('');
}
```

In this case we can check what the code is probably doing using our common knowledge in programming:

- The method `split` probably converts a string into an array.
- The method `reverse` probably reverses the contents of an array.
- The method `join` probably converts an array into a string.

This already looks good. However, if we want to be sure and we do not know the methods used in the code, we can check what each method does from a reliable source, such as the MDN Web Docs. After that, we can try giving some inputs to the function and see what it returns:

4.4 AI Content Accuracy

```
> reverseString("abc")
'cba'
> reverseString("hello")
'olleh'
> reverseString("a")
'a'
```

This also looks good because the function returns the correct answer in each test. Based on this, we could probably use the function in our code without problems.

A more difficult situation is when the answer is not a piece of code that we could simply analyze and test. For example, consider the following prompt:

> *Prompt*: I'm using PHP to create a web application. What is a safe way to store passwords in a database?
>
> *Answer*: A safe way to store passwords in a database is to hash them using PHP's built-in `password_hash()` function. This function applies a strong, one-way hashing algorithm (like bcrypt) and automatically handles salt generation. When verifying a password during login, use `password_verify()`.
> Example:
>
> ```
> // Storing the password
> $hash = password_hash($password, PASSWORD_DEFAULT);
>
> // Verifying the password
> if (password_verify($enteredPassword, $hash)) {
>     // Password is correct
> }
> ```

In this case we cannot know how safe the suggested solution is by testing or looking at the code. It would be a bad idea to use this PHP code just because AI recommended it. Instead, we can see the AI's suggestion as a possible option worth looking into more closely. For example, it would be good to look for more information about the following things:

- How does the `password_hash` function work more precisely?
- Is it still recommended to use this function? (AI tools do not always have up-to-date information.)
- What does the `PASSWORD_DEFAULT` parameter mean?
- What does it mean that the hashing algorithm is strong? How strong is it?
- What does salt generation mean?
- How does automatic salt generation work?
- For which use cases is the function safe enough?
- For which use cases is the function not safe enough?
- What other possible approaches are there?

Note that the length of the list above does not mean that AI-generated content is necessarily especially unreliable. It is always important to check information, no matter what the source is. However, as AI tools often give direct answers to questions using convincing language, their answers may seem more reliable than, for example, answers found on a website through a search engine.

But how reliable are AI-generated answers? In a study, researchers collected a set of programming-related questions from Stack Overflow and posed them to ChatGPT, which gave incorrect information in more than half of the cases [1]. Does this mean we should keep using good old Stack Overflow instead of ChatGPT?

The situation is not as simple as just choosing one of them. Stack Overflow and ChatGPT are different ways to seek help. ChatGPT gives an answer instantly, without having to wait for a human response. It is expected that somewhere in the world, there is a human programmer who can give a better answer than ChatGPT to a specific question. However, it is not clear when such an answer will be posted to a new Stack Overflow question, or if it will be posted at all. Even if AI-generated answers may contain mistakes, they can still be useful.

This is not the first time that a new way to search for information has raised doubts. In the early 2000s, when Wikipedia started, there was much discussion about whether such an open encyclopedia could be trusted. In 2005, the journal Nature compared articles from Wikipedia and Encyclopaedia Britannica, and found that the differences in accuracy were surprisingly small [2]. Encyclopaedia Britannica did not accept the results and demanded Nature to retract the article.

Today we know that Wikipedia is definitely a useful source of information, even though anyone can edit its articles. Over the years, we have learned what the role of Wikipedia is and in which situations we can use it. We should not trust the information on Wikipedia, but it is often a valuable starting point, and we can use other sources to verify the information. In the future, we will also know more about the best ways to use AI for information searching.

References

1. S. Kabir, D. N. Udo-Imeh, B. Kou, T. Zhang, Is stack overflow obsolete? an empirical study of the characteristics of ChatGPT answers to Stack Overflow questions, in *CHI Conference on Human Factors in Computing Systems* (2024)
2. J. Giles, Internet encyclopaedias go head to head. Nature **438**, 900–901 (2005)

Code Generation 5

This chapter discusses the use of AI tools in code generation, which is a common way to apply generative AI in programming. While AI tools can automatically create code, the expertise of programmers is still important in the process.

Section 5.1 explores prompting techniques related to code generation. In general, the more relevant information we include in the prompt, the better the quality of the generated code. We also give examples of creating code based on existing data.

Section 5.2 discusses the accuracy of AI-generated code. While it is often easy to test if the code works at all, there can be more subtle issues that are harder to detect. It is also difficult to evaluate how well AI tools generate code in general.

Section 5.3 provides more examples of code creation using AI tools. In addition to program code, we can generate shell scripts, regular expressions, and SQL commands. Another use of AI tools is generating user interface code by using images as prompts.

Section 5.4 focuses on a phenomenon called vibe coding, where the goal is to generate code with AI tools without a deep understanding of how the code works. With vibe coding, people who have limited programming knowledge can try to create applications.

5.1 Prompting Techniques

5.1.1 First Example

Suppose we need a JavaScript function that checks if a given password is valid using some criteria. We can use the following prompt to generate the code:

Prompt: Create a JavaScript function `validPassword` that checks if a given password is valid. The password should contain at least 8 characters, both lowercase and uppercase characters, and at least one digit.

Answer: You can create a JavaScript function called `validPassword` that checks if a given password meets the specified criteria. Below is an implementation of this function:

```javascript
function validPassword(password) {
    // Check the length of the password
    if (password.length < 8) {
        return false;
    }

    // Initialize flags for lowercase, uppercase, and digit
    let hasLowercase = false;
    let hasUppercase = false;
    let hasDigit = false;

    // Check each character in the password
    for (let char of password) {
        if (char >= 'a' && char <= 'z') {
            hasLowercase = true;
        } else if (char >= 'A' && char <= 'Z') {
            hasUppercase = true;
        } else if (char >= '0' && char <= '9') {
            hasDigit = true;
        }

        // If all conditions are met, no need to continue checking
        if (hasLowercase && hasUppercase && hasDigit) {
            return true;
        }
    }

    // Return true only if all conditions are satisfied
    return hasLowercase && hasUppercase && hasDigit;
}
```

After generating the code, we should not assume directly that the code works, but instead read through the code and test it. The code above seems to work, but there are a few areas for improvement.

First, in every iteration of the for loop, the code checks three flag variables and returns true if all the flags are true. The purpose of this check is probably to avoid running the loop longer than necessary, but this can be seen as an unnecessary optimization that makes the code more complex.

Second, the code includes comments that are not really needed because it is easy to understand what the code does without them. AI tools often add many comments that explain each section of the code, which can be helpful for learning programming, but may not be preferred in other situations.

Let's use another prompt to improve the code:

5.1 Prompting Techniques

Prompt: Please remove the comments and also check the flags only after the loop.

Answer: Here's the `validPassword` function without comments and checking the flags only after the loop:

```javascript
function validPassword(password) {
    if (password.length < 8) {
        return false;
    }

    let hasLowercase = false;
    let hasUppercase = false;
    let hasDigit = false;

    for (let char of password) {
        if (char >= 'a' && char <= 'z') {
            hasLowercase = true;
        } else if (char >= 'A' && char <= 'Z') {
            hasUppercase = true;
        } else if (char >= '0' && char <= '9') {
            hasDigit = true;
        }
    }

    return hasLowercase && hasUppercase && hasDigit;
}
```

Of course, if we want to modify AI-generated code, we can also do it ourselves instead of asking the AI to make the changes. It can be easier and more efficient to edit the code directly rather than describing the changes and then checking the results. In the case above, it would probably have been faster to remove the unnecessary checks in the loop ourselves instead of asking the AI to do it.

5.1.2 Specifying Requirements

If we don't clearly specify the requirements in our code, AI tools tend to guess what the requirements could be. For example, consider the following prompt:

Prompt: Generate a Python function that is given a text file name. The function finds all email addresses in the file and returns them as a list.

Answer: Here's a Python function to extract all email addresses from a given text file using regular expressions:

```python
import re

def extract_emails_from_file(filename):
    pattern = r'[a-zA-Z0-9_.+-]+@[a-zA-Z0-9-]+\.[a-zA-Z0-9-.]+'
    emails = []
    with open(filename, 'r', encoding='utf-8') as f:
        text = f.read()
        emails = re.findall(pattern, text)
    return emails
```

As we didn't specify the format of an email address, the AI just generated a regular expression that sets some requirements for the address. The problem is that defining the exact format of an email address is often a bad idea because it is easy to miss special cases. Instead, we could simply consider all strings that contain exactly one @ character as possible email addresses.

Also, we didn't specify what should happen if the same email address appears several times in the file. The function above reports duplicate addresses, but it might be better to report only unique addresses.

Here is an improved prompt that more clearly specifies what we want to do:

Prompt: Generate a Python function that is given a text file name. The function finds all email addresses in the file and returns them as a list.

Here any string that contains exactly one character @ and doesn't contain whitespace is regarded as an email address. Don't use regular expressions in the function. The return list should consist of unique addresses.

Answer: Here's a Python function that follows your requirements:

```python
def find_emails(filename):
    emails = set()
    with open(filename, 'r', encoding='utf-8') as f:
        for line in f:
            tokens = line.strip().split()
            for token in tokens:
                if token.count('@') == 1:
                    emails.add(token)
    return list(emails)
```

By using a more precise prompt, we obtained a function that better matches our requirements. This is a good general technique for creating prompts: clearly state your requirements, as this often improves the quality of the generated code.

While AI tools usually do not ask follow-up questions even if our requirements are unclear, we can use a prompt that asks them to request clarifications about our requirements before creating code:

5.1 Prompting Techniques

Prompt: Generate a Python function that is given a text file name. The function finds all email addresses in the file and returns them as a list.

However, before creating the function, ask me for more details about my requirements. Don't make assumptions.

Answer: Absolutely! Before I write the function, could you please clarify a few details:
1. Email Format: Should the function only match standard email formats, or do you want to support more complex/rare formats (e.g., emails with subdomains, plus signs, etc.)?
2. Case Sensitivity: Should the email search be case-sensitive or case-insensitive?
3. Duplicates: Should the returned list include duplicate email addresses if they appear multiple times, or should it only return unique emails?
4. File Size: Will the files be large (e.g., hundreds of MBs), or can I assume they are small enough to read into memory at once?
5. Output: Should the function return the emails in the order they appear, or is any order acceptable?
6. Invalid Emails: Should the function attempt to validate emails beyond the pattern (e.g., check for valid domain extensions), or is a simple pattern match enough?
7. Error Handling: How should the function handle cases where the file does not exist or cannot be read?

Let me know your preferences on these points!

Prompt: Here are my answers:
1. Any string that contains exactly one @ character and no whitespace
2. Case-insensitive
3. Only unique emails
4. You can assume the file is quite small
5. Any order is fine
6. No validation required
7. You can just assume that the file exists

Answer: Great! Here is the Python function based on your requirements:

```python
import re

def extract_emails(filename):
    email_pattern = re.compile(r'\S+@\S+', re.IGNORECASE)
    emails = set()
    with open(filename, 'r', encoding='utf-8') as f:
        for line in f:
            for candidate in email_pattern.findall(line):
                if candidate.count('@') == 1:
                    emails.add(candidate.lower())
    return list(emails)
```

5.1.3 Simplifying Code

AI tools often generate code that is complex and include elements that are not actually needed. Let's consider the following example, where we want to generate a simple HTML page that shows the number of days until New Year 2026.

Prompt: Can you create a simple HTML page that shows the number of days until New Year 2026?

Answer: Below is a simple HTML page that uses JavaScript to calculate and display the number of days remaining until New Year 2026. You can copy and paste this code into an HTML file and open it in a web browser to see it in action.

```html
<!DOCTYPE html>
<html lang="en">
<head>
    <meta charset="UTF-8">
    <meta name="viewport"
        content="width=device-width, initial-scale=1.0">
    <title>Days Until New Year 2026</title>
    <style>
        body {
            font-family: Arial, sans-serif;
            text-align: center;
            margin-top: 50px;
        }
        .countdown {
            font-size: 2em;
            color: #2c3e50;
        }
    </style>
</head>
<body>
    <h1>Countdown to New Year 2026</h1>
    <div class="countdown" id="countdown"></div>

    <script>
        function calculateDaysUntilNewYear() {
            const today = new Date();
            const newYear2026 = new Date('2026-01-01');
            const timeDifference = newYear2026 - today;
            const daysRemaining =
                Math.ceil(timeDifference / (1000 * 60 * 60 * 24));

            return daysRemaining;
        }

        document.getElementById('countdown').innerText =
            calculateDaysUntilNewYear() + ' days remaining!';
    </script>
</body>
</html>
```

The first version of the HTML code contains CSS styles and other elements that are actually not needed. We can simplify the code as follows:

5.1 Prompting Techniques

Prompt: Please simplify the code. Remove CSS and anything else that is not really needed.

Answer: Here's a simplified version of the HTML page that focuses solely on the functionality of counting down the days until New Year 2026, without any additional styling or unnecessary elements:

```html
<!DOCTYPE html>
<html lang="en">
<head>
    <meta charset="UTF-8">
    <title>Days Until New Year 2026</title>
</head>
<body>
    <h1>Countdown to New Year 2026</h1>
    <div id="countdown"></div>

    <script>
        const today = new Date();
        const newYear2026 = new Date('2026-01-01');
        const timeDifference = newYear2026 - today;
        const daysRemaining =
            Math.ceil(timeDifference / (1000 * 60 * 60 * 24));
        document.getElementById('countdown').innerText =
            daysRemaining + ' days remaining!';
    </script>
</body>
</html>
```

The new code is simpler than the first version, but it still contains some elements that are not really necessary. We can continue the process by using another prompt. In this situation, a good technique is to give instructions on what changes could be made to further simplify the code.

Prompt: Can you still simplify the code? You can leave out some HTML elements and perhaps simplify the JavaScript code as well.

Answer: Here's an even more simplified version of the HTML page. This version minimizes the HTML structure and condenses the JavaScript code:

```html
<!DOCTYPE html>
<html>
<body>
    <h1>Days Until New Year 2026</h1>
    <div id="countdown"></div>

    <script>
        const timeDifference = new Date('2026-01-01') - new Date();
        const daysRemaining =
            Math.ceil(timeDifference / (1000 * 60 * 60 * 24));
        document.getElementById('countdown').innerText =
            daysRemaining + ' days remaining!';
    </script>
</body>
</html>
```

5.1.4 Programming Style

If we do not give instructions about the code style, AI will use a default style that has formed during its training. This can especially be noticed in programming languages that do not have one established style. As an example, consider the following example that generates a C function:

> *Prompt*: Create a C function that finds the maximum difference between two numbers in the given int array.
>
> *Answer*: Below is a simple C function that finds the maximum difference between any two elements in the given array.
>
> ```c
> int maxDifference(int arr[], int n) {
>     if (n < 2) return 0; // Not enough elements for a difference
>
>     int minElement = arr[0];
>     int maxDiff = arr[1] - arr[0];
>
>     for (int i = 1; i < n; i++) {
>         if (arr[i] - minElement > maxDiff) {
>             maxDiff = arr[i] - minElement;
>         }
>         if (arr[i] < minElement) {
>             minElement = arr[i];
>         }
>     }
>     return maxDiff;
> }
> ```

This answer follows a specific C programming style, where the indentation size is four spaces, and the camel case naming style (for example, `minElement` instead of `min_element`) is used. However, we can change the programming style by giving more precise instructions in the prompt:

> *Prompt*: You are an experienced C programmer who follows the Linux kernel coding style. Create a C function that finds the maximum difference of two numbers in the given int array.
>
> *Answer*: Here is a C function that finds the maximum difference between any two numbers in the given array.
>
> ```c
> int max_difference(int *arr, int n)
> {
>         int i, min, max;
>
>         if (n < 2)
>                 return -1; /* Not enough elements */
>
>         min = INT_MAX;
>         max = INT_MIN;
>
>         for (i = 0; i < n; i++) {
>                 if (arr[i] < min)
> ```

```
                    min = arr[i];
        if (arr[i] > max)
                    max = arr[i];
    }

    return max - min;
}
```

5.1.5 Data-Based Generation

In some cases, it can be convenient to use AI tools to generate code based on existing data. This can involve changing the format of the data so that it can be included in the code, or generating more data based on an example.

For example, suppose we have a two-dimensional maze in textual format and we want to create Python code that stores the maze in a list structure. In this situation, we can use the following prompt:

Prompt: Consider the following maze:

```
##########
#...#...#B#
#.#.#.#.#.#
#A#...#...#
##########
```

Create a Python code that defines this maze as a list of lists where each element is a single character.

Answer: You can represent the given maze as a list of lists in Python, where each inner list corresponds to a row in the maze. Here's how you can define the maze:

```
maze = [
    ['#', '#', '#', '#', '#', '#', '#', '#', '#', '#', '#'],
    ['#', '.', '.', '.', '#', '.', '.', '.', '#', 'B', '#'],
    ['#', '.', '#', '.', '#', '.', '#', '.', '#', '.', '#'],
    ['#', 'A', '#', '.', '.', '.', '#', '.', '.', '.', '#'],
    ['#', '#', '#', '#', '#', '#', '#', '#', '#', '#', '#']
]
```

Here, we avoided manual work by automatically converting the textual maze representation into Python code. However, we should check that the converted maze matches the original maze.

As another example, consider the task of creating a list that contains every month of the year along with the number of days in each month. In this situation, we can start by adding the first month, January, to the list and ask AI to do the rest:

> *Prompt*: Here is the first line of code. Add the other months following this example.
>
> ```
> months.add("January", 31);
> ```
>
> *Answer*: Based on the example you provided for January, here are the corresponding lines of code for the other months, including their respective number of days:
>
> ```
> months.add("January", 31);
> months.add("February", 28);  // 29 for leap years
> months.add("March", 31);
> months.add("April", 30);
> months.add("May", 31);
> months.add("June", 30);
> months.add("July", 31);
> months.add("August", 31);
> months.add("September", 30);
> months.add("October", 31);
> months.add("November", 30);
> months.add("December", 31);
> ```
>
> Note: February has 28 days in a common year and 29 days in a leap year, so you may want to handle that condition separately in your code if necessary.

5.2 Code Generation Accuracy

As we have discussed in previous chapters, we should never automatically assume that we can directly use AI-generated code. There is always a possibility that the code does something unexpected. An easy situation for us is when we notice that the code does not work at all. The code may simply be wrong, or it may assume that we are using a different language version or compiler.

A more difficult situation is when the code *seems* to work but still has subtle issues. Perhaps we have not specified something clearly enough, or the AI has misunderstood our requirements. In particular, it is possible that the code is just a simple example and not meant to be used directly in a real application. For example, consider the following Java code that reads an integer from the standard input:

```
Scanner scanner = new Scanner(System.in);
int number = scanner.nextInt();
```

This code works when the user gives an integer that fits the `int` data type. Otherwise, the code generates an `InputMismatchException` which could be handled as follows:

```
Scanner scanner = new Scanner(System.in);
try {
    int number = scanner.nextInt();
} catch (InputMismatchException e) {
    // ...
}
```

5.2 Code Generation Accuracy

In a study [1], researchers created a dataset of Stack Overflow questions related to using Java libraries. They found that in 62% of cases, AI-generated answers had issues, such as not handling exceptions that may occur in certain situations, like in the code above. This does not mean that code without exception handling is strictly incorrect, but it has an issue that can cause problems in real applications.

Again, it should be remembered that just because a human programmer has written some code, it does not guarantee that the code is free from issues. In a study related to code security [2], it was found that AI-generated code contained 20% *fewer* vulnerabilities compared to Stack Overflow answers. However, there were still many issues in both AI-generated and Stack Overflow answers.

One of the first achievements in AI code generation were impressive results in programming contests [3]. Later, LeetCode problems have been used to evaluate AI code generation accuracy. LeetCode is a website that provides programming contest style problems with well-specified input and output requirements. The problems are divided into three difficulty categories: easy, medium, and hard. For example, here is the problem statement for a problem called *Two Sum*[1] :

> Given an array of integers nums and an integer target, return indices of the two numbers such that they add up to target.
>
> You may assume that each input would have exactly one solution, and you may not use the same element twice.
>
> You can return the answer in any order.

The problem statements also include example inputs and outputs. For the problem above, one of the examples is as follows:

```
Input: nums = [2,7,11,15], target = 9
Output: [0,1]
Explanation: Because nums[0] + nums[1] == 9, we return [0, 1]
```

Interestingly, it has been reported that ChatGPT can solve LeetCode problems published before its knowledge cutoff much better than those published after it. In a study [4], ChatGPT correctly solved 90, 71, and 40% of the easy, medium, and hard problems published before the knowledge cutoff, but only 52, 14, and 1% of those published after the knowledge cutoff. It is possible that LeetCode problems and their solutions have been included in the ChatGPT training data, and earlier problems may be easier to solve because ChatGPT has already "seen" them.

It is difficult to make general statements about how accurately AI tools generate code because there are so many different contexts. For example, it is straightforward to evaluate performance on LeetCode problems that have well-defined inputs and outputs, but these problems may be very different from real software development. Also, an AI tool might generate high-quality code for a specific programming language or framework but may not produce good results in another context.

---

[1] https://leetcode.com/problems/two-sum/.

5.3 Further Examples

5.3.1 Shell Script Generation

Automatically creating custom shell scripts can be very useful, as many programmers are not used to writing them. As an example, suppose we have a collection of PNG image files that we want to resize and rename. Let's ask for instructions on how to do this automatically using Unix tools:

> *Prompt*: I have a large number of PNG files. Create a Unix shell script that converts each image to the size 320 x 200 pixels and gives them names 001.png, 002.png, etc.
>
> *Answer*: Here's a shell script that accomplishes this using ImageMagick's convert:
>
> ```
> #!/bin/bash
> 
> count=1
> 
> # Find all PNG files (case-insensitive), sorted by name
> for file in $(ls *.png *.PNG 2>/dev/null | sort); do
>     # Format the output filename as 3 digits, e.g., 001.png
>     out=$(printf "%03d.png" "$count")
>     # Convert and resize
>     convert "$file" -resize 320x200\! "$out"
>     count=$((count + 1))
> done
> ```

The script above uses a loop that goes through the PNG files in the current directory. Each file is converted using ImageMagick, and a counter variable is used to generate new file names.

5.3.2 Regular Expression Generation

Consider the task of creating a regular expression that matches time strings that have the format HH:MM:SS, where HH is the hour between 00 and 23, MM is minutes between 00 and 59, and SS is seconds between 00 and 59.

> *Prompt*: Generate a regular expression that checks that the given string has the format "HH:MM:SS".
>
> *Answer*: To create a regular expression that checks if a given string follows the format "HH:MM:SS", you can use the following pattern:
>
> ```
> ^(?:[01]\d|2[0-3]):[0-5]\d:[0-5]\d$
> ```

A more difficult challenge is to create a regular expression that matches date strings with the format YYYY-MM-DD where YYYY is the year, MM is the month between 01 and 12 and DD is the day between 01 and 31. Here the difficulty is that the number of days in a month depends on the month, and the number of days in February also depends on the year.

> *Prompt*: Generate a regular expression that checks that the given string has the format "YYYY-MM-DD".
>
> *Answer*: To create a regular expression that checks if a string is in the format "YYYY-MM-DD", you can use the following regex pattern:
>
> ```
> ^\d{4}-(0[1-9]|1[0-2])-(0[1-9]|[12]\d|3[01])$
> ```

The resulting regular expression assumes that each month has 31 days and does not pay attention to leap years, which can be a good decision in practice. We could use a regular expression to first check that the format of the string is roughly correct, and after that use another method for checking that the string actually represents a valid date.

5.3.3 SQL Generation

In the following example, we include the schema of our database in the prompt, and generate a SQL query that fetches the list of threads:

> *Prompt*: Here is the schema of my database:
>
> ```sql
> CREATE TABLE users (
>     id INTEGER PRIMARY KEY,
>     username TEXT,
>     password TEXT
> );
> CREATE TABLE threads (
>     id INTEGER PRIMARY KEY,
>     subject TEXT,
>     content TEXT,
>     user_id INTEGER,
>     created_at TIMESTAMP,
>     FOREIGN KEY (user_id) REFERENCES users(id)
> );
> CREATE TABLE messages (
>     id INTEGER PRIMARY KEY,
>     content TEXT,
>     user_id INTEGER,
>     thread_id INTEGER,
>     created_at TIMESTAMP,
>     FOREIGN KEY (user_id) REFERENCES users(id),
>     FOREIGN KEY (thread_id) REFERENCES threads(id)
> );
> ```
>
> Create a SQL query that fetches the list of threads. For each thread, include the subject, the number of messages, and information of the latest message (sender, timestamp). Before creating the query, please ask for details from me.
>
> *Answer*: Absolutely! Before I create the SQL query, I need a few clarifications:
> - Sender Information: For the "sender" of the latest message, do you want just the sender's `username`, or do you want more details (like their `id`, etc.)?

- Threads with No Messages: Should threads without any messages be included in the result? If so, what should be displayed for the latest message fields (NULL, empty, etc.)?
- Ordering: Do you want the threads ordered in any particular way (e.g., by creation date, by latest message time, etc.)?
- Pagination: Should the query support pagination (LIMIT/OFFSET), or return all threads?
- Other Fields: Besides subject, number of messages, and latest message info, do you want any other thread or user fields included?

Let me know your preferences!

Prompt: Here are my answers:

1. Include both sender id and username
2. You can assume that each thread has at least one message
3. Order the threads from newest to oldest (you can use the id field)
4. No pagination needed
5. Also include thread id

Answer: Thank you for the clarifications! Here's the SQL query to accomplish this:

```sql
SELECT
    t.id AS thread_id,
    t.subject,
    COUNT(m.id) AS message_count,
    lm.user_id AS latest_message_user_id,
    u.username AS latest_message_username,
    lm.created_at AS latest_message_created_at
FROM
    threads t
JOIN
    messages m ON m.thread_id = t.id
JOIN (
    -- Get the latest message (by max id) for each thread
    SELECT
        thread_id,
        MAX(id) AS max_message_id
    FROM
        messages
    GROUP BY
        thread_id
) lm_id ON lm_id.thread_id = t.id
JOIN
    messages lm ON lm.id = lm_id.max_message_id
JOIN
    users u ON u.id = lm.user_id
GROUP BY
    t.id, t.subject, lm.user_id, u.username, lm.created_at
ORDER BY
    t.id DESC;
```

5.3.4 Image-Based Generation

Some AI tools also support creating code by using images in our prompts. This can be useful, for example, when we want to generate code for creating a user interface. In this case, we can *draw* a sketch of the user interface and automatically generate code that creates such a user interface.

As an example, let's generate Python code that shows a dialog sketched in Fig. 5.1. The dialog should have a text box where the user can enter their name, and two buttons with captions "Continue" and "Cancel". To create the user interface, we would like to use the Tkinter library which is included in the Python standard library. Let's use the following prompt with the image attached:

5.3 Further Examples

Fig. 5.1 Sketch for our user interface

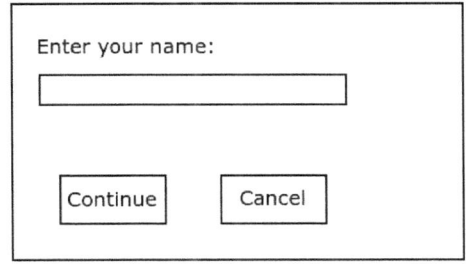

Prompt: Create a Python/Tkinter application that shows the dialog in the attached image.

Answer: Here's a Python script using `tkinter` that replicates the dialog shown in your image:

```
import tkinter as tk
from tkinter import messagebox

def on_continue():
    name = name_entry.get()
    messagebox.showinfo("Info", f"Hello, {name}!")

def on_cancel():
    root.destroy()

# Create the main window
root = tk.Tk()
root.title("Name Entry")
root.geometry("300x150")
root.resizable(False, False)

# Label
label = tk.Label(root, text="Enter your name:")
label.pack(pady=(15, 5))

# Entry box
name_entry = tk.Entry(root, width=30)
name_entry.pack()

# Button frame
button_frame = tk.Frame(root)
button_frame.pack(pady=20)

# Continue button
continue_button = tk.Button(button_frame, text="Continue", command=
    on_continue, width=10)
continue_button.pack(side=tk.LEFT, padx=10)

# Cancel button
cancel_button = tk.Button(button_frame, text="Cancel", command=
    on_cancel, width=10)
cancel_button.pack(side=tk.LEFT, padx=10)

# Run the application
root.mainloop()
```

Fig. 5.2 Our user interface created using the Tkinter library in Python

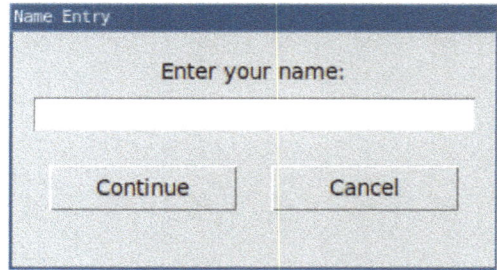

Figure 5.2 shows the result when we run the code. This dialog matches our sketch, and the code also includes functions for handling the events when the user presses the buttons.

Then, let's use the same image to create a HTML page that shows the dialog using JavaScript:

Prompt: Create an HTML/JavaScript page that shows the dialog in the attached image.

Answer: Here's a simple HTML and JavaScript page that recreates the dialog from the image you provided:

```html
<!DOCTYPE html>
<html lang="en">
<head>
  <meta charset="UTF-8">
  <title>Name Input Dialog</title>
  <style>
    [...]
  </style>
</head>
<body>

<div class="dialog-box">
  <label for="nameInput">Enter your name:</label>
  <input type="text" id="nameInput" />

  <div class="buttons">
    <button onclick="onContinue()">Continue</button>
    <button onclick="onCancel()">Cancel</button>
  </div>
</div>

<script>
  function onContinue() {
    const name = document.getElementById('nameInput').value;
    alert("Hello, " + name + "!");
  }
```

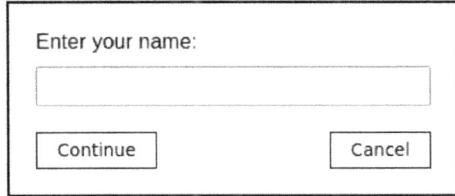

Fig. 5.3 Our user interface created using HTML and JavaScript

```
    function onCancel() {
      document.getElementById('nameInput').value = "";
    }
  </script>

  </body>
</html>
```

Figure 5.3 shows the result of the above code (note that the CSS part is omitted to save space). Again, the result matches our sketch. This time, JavaScript is used to handle the events when the user presses the buttons.

5.4 Vibe Coding

The term *vibe coding* refers to a process where a person uses generative AI to create code without much understanding of how the code works. For example, someone who is not a programmer, or does not care about the actual code, gives instructions to an AI tool.

The first step in vibe coding is to describe the code that should be implemented. In many cases, the first version created by AI does not work correctly and needs fixes. If the code does not work at all and gives an error message, the vibe coder can forward the error message to the AI and request a fix. Sometimes there are no errors, but the functionality of the code is not correct. In this case, the vibe coder can report the problem and ask the AI to fix it.

Vibe coding can be seen as a problematic programming technique. If we do not understand what we are doing, it may be difficult or impossible to create a working application or extend it later. If the code is a black box that nobody has checked, it can even be dangerous to use. On the other hand, vibe coding may be useful in situations where the quality of the code is not important. For example, we may need some throwaway code for demonstration purposes, and we know that the code will not be used or maintained later.

As an example, let's try to create a small game using vibe coding. The idea is to combine two ingredients: the classic Pong game and an analog clock.

> *Prompt*: Create a two-player pong game using Python/Pygame where the ball is replaced with an analog clock.
>
> *Answer*: Creating a two-player Pong game using Python and Pygame where the ball is replaced with an analog clock is a fun and interesting challenge. Below is a complete implementation of this concept. Before running the code, ensure you have Pygame installed. Here's the code for the game: [...]

The first version of the code does not work at all: when we try to run it, we get an error message saying that the code tries to use an unassigned variable. In this case, we can forward the error message to the AI.

> *Prompt*: I tried to run the code but get the following error. Can you fix it?
>
> ```
> UnboundLocalError: local variable 'paddle1_pos' referenced before
>     assignment}
> ```
>
> *Answer*: The error you're encountering typically occurs when you try to modify a variable inside a function without declaring it as `global`. In this case, the `paddle1_pos` and `paddle2_pos` variables are being modified within the main loop without being declared as global. To fix this issue, you can declare these variables as global at the beginning of the `main` function. Here's the corrected code: [...]

After the fix, there are no errors and the game starts, but it still does not work properly. The clock, which should act as the ball, does not move at all.

> *Prompt*: The game works but the ball is not moving. Can you fix that?
>
> *Answer*: In the original implementation, the game was designed to replace the ball with an analog clock, which means there was no actual ball movement logic. To create a more interactive experience, we can add functionality that simulates the movement of the clock in a bouncing manner, similar to how a ball would move in a traditional Pong game.
>
> Here's the updated code that includes a clock that moves around the screen and bounces off the paddles and walls: [...]

Now the game works much better, and the ball bounces when it hits the top or bottom wall. However, the ball does not bounce when it hits the left or right paddle.

> *Prompt*: There is still a problem: the ball doesn't bounce when it hits the left or right paddle. Can you fix that?
>
> *Answer*: To ensure that the clock (acting as the ball) bounces off the paddles correctly, we need to refine the collision detection logic. The current implementation checks for collisions but may not correctly handle the conditions for bouncing off the paddles.
>
> Here's the updated code that correctly detects collisions with the paddles and ensures the clock bounces off them: [...]

5.4 Vibe Coding

Fig. 5.4 Analog clock pong game created using vibe coding

Unfortunately, we don't get the full code for the game anymore. The reason for this could be that the code is too long for the AI tool to generate. A trick that sometimes helps is to ask for a shorter version of the code. Using this trick, we finally get code that works as expected (Fig. 5.4):

Prompt: For some reason, you provided only part of the code. Can you present the whole code in a shorter form?

Answer: Here's the complete code presented in a more concise format while maintaining readability:

```python
import pygame
import sys
import math
import time

# Initialize Pygame
pygame.init()

# Constants
WIDTH, HEIGHT = 800, 600
PADDLE_WIDTH, PADDLE_HEIGHT = 10, 100
CLOCK_RADIUS = 40
WHITE = (255, 255, 255)
BLACK = (0, 0, 0)
FPS = 60

# Set up the display
screen = pygame.display.set_mode((WIDTH, HEIGHT))
pygame.display.set_caption("Pong with Analog Clock")

# Paddle and clock positions
paddle1_pos = [30, HEIGHT // 2 - PADDLE_HEIGHT // 2]
paddle2_pos = [WIDTH - 30 - PADDLE_WIDTH,
        HEIGHT // 2 - PADDLE_HEIGHT // 2]
clock_pos = [WIDTH // 2, HEIGHT // 2]
clock_velocity = [5, 5]  # Initial velocity for the clock

# Function to draw the analog clock
def draw_clock(surface, position):
```

```python
    current_time = time.localtime()
    hour_angle = math.radians((current_time.tm_hour % 12 +
        current_time.tm_min / 60) * 30 - 90)
    minute_angle = math.radians((current_time.tm_min +
        current_time.tm_sec / 60) * 6 - 90)
    second_angle = math.radians(current_time.tm_sec * 6 - 90)

    # Draw clock face
    pygame.draw.circle(surface, WHITE, position, CLOCK_RADIUS)
    pygame.draw.circle(surface, BLACK, position, CLOCK_RADIUS, 2)
    pygame.draw.line(surface, BLACK, position,
        (position[0] + CLOCK_RADIUS * 0.5 * math.cos(hour_angle),
        position[1] + CLOCK_RADIUS * 0.5 * math.sin(hour_angle)), 6)
    pygame.draw.line(surface, BLACK, position,
        (position[0] + CLOCK_RADIUS * 0.7 * math.cos(minute_angle),
        position[1] + CLOCK_RADIUS * 0.7 * math.sin(minute_angle)), 4)
    pygame.draw.line(surface, (255, 0, 0), position,
        (position[0] + CLOCK_RADIUS * 0.9 * math.cos(second_angle),
        position[1] + CLOCK_RADIUS * 0.9 * math.sin(second_angle)), 2)

# Main game loop
def main():
    global paddle1_pos, paddle2_pos
    clock = pygame.time.Clock()
    paddle1_speed = paddle2_speed = 0

    while True:
        for event in pygame.event.get():
            if event.type == pygame.QUIT:
                pygame.quit()
                sys.exit()
            if event.type == pygame.KEYDOWN:
                if event.key == pygame.K_w: paddle1_speed = -5
                if event.key == pygame.K_s: paddle1_speed = 5
                if event.key == pygame.K_UP: paddle2_speed = -5
                if event.key == pygame.K_DOWN: paddle2_speed = 5
            if event.type == pygame.KEYUP:
                if event.key in (pygame.K_w, pygame.K_s):
                    paddle1_speed = 0
                if event.key in (pygame.K_UP, pygame.K_DOWN):
                    paddle2_speed = 0

        # Update paddle positions
        paddle1_pos[1] = max(0, min(HEIGHT - PADDLE_HEIGHT,
                                    paddle1_pos[1] + paddle1_speed))
        paddle2_pos[1] = max(0, min(HEIGHT - PADDLE_HEIGHT,
                                    paddle2_pos[1] + paddle2_speed))

        # Update clock position
        clock_pos[0] += clock_velocity[0]
        clock_pos[1] += clock_velocity[1]

        # Bounce off walls
        if clock_pos[1] - CLOCK_RADIUS <= 0 or \
           clock_pos[1] + CLOCK_RADIUS >= HEIGHT:
            clock_velocity[1] = -clock_velocity[1]

        # Bounce off paddles
        if (paddle1_pos[0] < clock_pos[0] - CLOCK_RADIUS <
                paddle1_pos[0] + PADDLE_WIDTH and
            paddle1_pos[1] < clock_pos[1] <
                paddle1_pos[1] + PADDLE_HEIGHT) or \
           (paddle2_pos[0] < clock_pos[0] + CLOCK_RADIUS <
                paddle2_pos[0] + PADDLE_WIDTH and
            paddle2_pos[1] < clock_pos[1] <
                paddle2_pos[1] + PADDLE_HEIGHT):
            clock_velocity[0] = -clock_velocity[0]
```

```
            # Clear the screen
            screen.fill(BLACK)

            # Draw paddles and clock
            pygame.draw.rect(screen, WHITE,
                (*paddle1_pos, PADDLE_WIDTH, PADDLE_HEIGHT))
            pygame.draw.rect(screen, WHITE,
                (*paddle2_pos, PADDLE_WIDTH, PADDLE_HEIGHT))
            draw_clock(screen, clock_pos)

            # Update the display
            pygame.display.flip()
            clock.tick(FPS)
if __name__ == "__main__":
    main()
```

References

1. L. Zhong, Z. Wang, Can LLM replace stack overflow? a study on robustness and reliability of large language model code generation, in *AAAI Conference on Artificial Intelligence* (2024)
2. S. Hamer, M. d'Amorim, L. Williams, Just another copy and paste? Comparing the security vulnerabilities of ChatGPT generated code and StackOverflow answers, in *IEEE Security and Privacy Workshops* (2024)
3. Y. Li, D. Choi, J. Chung et al., Competition-level code generation with AlphaCode. Science **378**(6624), 1092–1097 (2022)
4. Z. Liu, Y. Tang, X. Luo et al., No need to lift a finger anymore? Assessing the quality of code generation by ChatGPT. IEEE Trans. Softw. Eng. **50**(6), 1548–1584 (2024)

Testing Code

6

This chapter discusses the use of AI tools in code testing. Generative AI can be used both to test code directly, like a human tester, and to generate unit tests and other testing code that will be run separately.

Section 6.1 presents a simple way to test code with AI: we create a prompt that includes the code and ask if there are cases where the code does not work correctly. This approach is similar to a testing method where another programmer reviews the code and tries to check if it is correct.

Section 6.2 focuses on automatically creating unit tests. Unit test generation can be fully automatic, where AI designs the tests on its own, or supervised, where a human programmer guides the test design process.

Section 6.3 discusses another testing method where we automatically create a large number of tests to thoroughly test the code. We then compare the code being tested with a reference code to see if they produce the same results for each test.

Section 6.4 explores how AI tools can be used to automatically create user interface tests for a web application. The goal is to develop a test suite that simulates how a human would use the application through a web browser, such as by following links to different pages and filling out forms.

6.1 Code Inspection

One way to test code using AI is to simply include the code in the prompt and ask if the AI can find any bugs in it. In this approach, we don't use AI to generate tests for the code, but instead to directly test the code itself. Besides finding bugs, the AI may also suggest how to fix them.

As an example, consider a Python function that tries to check if a given number is prime. A positive integer n is prime if no integer between 2 and $n-1$ divides it. For example, 5, 11, and 29 are primes. The following function does not work correctly because it claims that any number less than 2 is prime, which is not true. Let's try to find this bug using AI.

Prompt: I have created the following function that should check if a given number is prime. Can you find any inputs where the function returns an incorrect result?

```
def is_prime(n):
    for i in range(2, n):
        if n % i == 0:
            return False
    return True
```

Answer: The function you provided has a couple of issues that may cause it to return incorrect results for certain inputs. Let's analyze it:

- Handling of numbers less than 2: The function does not handle cases where n is less than 2. By definition, prime numbers are greater than 1. If you pass in n = 0 or n = 1, the function will return True, which is incorrect.
- Handling of the number 2: The function will return True for n = 2, which is correct since 2 is a prime number. However, it would be more efficient to explicitly handle this case.
- Return value for negative numbers: The function does not account for negative numbers. Negative numbers are not prime, but the function will incorrectly return True for any negative number.
  Here are some specific inputs that will return incorrect results:

- is_prime(0) will return True (incorrect)
- is_prime(1) will return True (incorrect)
- is_prime(-5) will return True (incorrect)

To fix the function, you could add checks for these cases:

```
def is_prime(n):
    if n < 2:
        return False
    for i in range(2, n):
        if n % i == 0:
            return False
    return True
```

With this modification, the function will correctly return False for inputs less than 2.

The bug in the code was correctly identified, and the AI also provided a revised version of the function. With the added check for $n < 2$, the function should work correctly for all inputs. In the analysis, it is correctly pointed out that the function previously handled numbers less than two incorrectly, including negative numbers. It is also mentioned that handling $n = 2$ as a special case would be more efficient, which is true, but this suggestion is not related to a bug.

An interesting experiment is to use the same prompt again with the fixed code. Are there still any cases where the code does not work correctly?

6.1 Code Inspection

Prompt: I have created the following function that should check if a given number is prime. Can you find any inputs where the function returns an incorrect result?

```
def is_prime(n):
    if n < 2:
        return False
    for i in range(2, n):
        if n % i == 0:
            return False
    return True
```

Answer: The function you've implemented has a logical flaw that can lead to incorrect results for certain inputs. Specifically, it will return `True` for the
number 1, which is not a prime number. Let's analyze the function step by step:
1. The function checks if n is less than 2. If it is, it correctly returns `False` for numbers less than 2.
2. The function then enters a loop from 2 to n - 1 and checks if n is divisible by any of these numbers.
3. If it finds any divisor, it returns `False`, indicating that n is not prime.
4. If no divisors are found, it returns `True`, indicating that n is prime.

The flaw arises because the loop checks divisibility for all numbers from 2 up to n - 1. However, the function does not handle the case for n = 1 correctly.

This analysis does not make sense, because the identified problem with the input $n = 1$ does not exist. Since the function first checks if $n < 2$ and returns `False` in that case, it correctly processes the input $n = 1$. In fact, the answer contains hallucination, as it claims both that the function returns `True` for the number 1 and that it returns `False` for numbers less than 2.

This behavior is typical of AI tools: if we ask them to find a bug in the code, they often assume that there must be a bug and they may even invent bugs. Therefore, we should always make sure that any "bug" found in the code is real before trying to fix it.

If we use the same prompt with the correct code several times, we may get different bug reports. For example:

Prompt: I have created the following function that should check if a given number is prime. Can you find any inputs where the function returns an incorrect result?

```
def is_prime(n):
    if n < 2:
        return False
    for i in range(2, n):
        if n % i == 0:
            return False
    return True
```

Answer: Your `is_prime` function has a logical flaw that can cause it to return incorrect results for certain inputs. Specifically, it does not handle the case when n is 2 correctly in the loop.
Here's a breakdown of the issues:
1. Loop Range: The loop iterates from 2 to n - 1. This means that if n is 2, the loop will not run at all because the range will be `range(2, 2)`, which is empty. As a result, the function will return `True`, which is correct for 2, but it may lead to confusion when considering other inputs.
2. Non-prime Numbers: The function will return `False` for any composite number correctly, but it could be misleading if the input is 1 or negative numbers, where it should return `False`.
3. Negative Numbers and Zero: The function correctly returns `False` for any number less than 2, which is good. However, it's important to note that negative numbers and zero are not prime.

This time the analysis first claims that the function does not work correctly with $n = 2$, but later mentions that the function will give the correct return value True but "it may lead to confusion when considering other inputs". It is not clear what this part of the analysis means.

6.2 Unit Test Generation
6.2.1 Primality Check

Instead of analyzing whether a piece of code works, we can also let AI create unit tests for the code. As an example, let's generate unit tests for the previously discussed primality check function:

> *Prompt*: I have created a Python function is_prime(n) that should check if the given number is prime. Can you create unit tests for the function?
>
> *Answer*: Here are some unit tests for the is_prime(n) function using the unittest framework in Python:
>
> ```python
> import unittest
>
> class TestIsPrime(unittest.TestCase):
>     def test_prime_numbers(self):
>         self.assertTrue(is_prime(2))
>         self.assertTrue(is_prime(3))
>         self.assertTrue(is_prime(5))
>         self.assertTrue(is_prime(7))
>         self.assertTrue(is_prime(11))
>         self.assertTrue(is_prime(13))
>         self.assertTrue(is_prime(17))
>
>     def test_non_prime_numbers(self):
>         self.assertFalse(is_prime(1))
>         self.assertFalse(is_prime(4))
>         self.assertFalse(is_prime(6))
>         self.assertFalse(is_prime(8))
>         self.assertFalse(is_prime(9))
>         self.assertFalse(is_prime(10))
>         self.assertFalse(is_prime(12))
>
>     def test_negative_numbers(self):
>         self.assertFalse(is_prime(-1))
>         self.assertFalse(is_prime(-10))
>
>     def test_edge_cases(self):
>         self.assertFalse(is_prime(0))
>         self.assertFalse(is_prime(-5))
>
> if __name__ == '__main__':
>     unittest.main()
> ```
>
> These tests cover various cases, including prime numbers, non-prime numbers, negative numbers, and edge cases.

6.2 Unit Test Generation

This test suite is a good initial test suite for the `is_prime` function. The test suite includes a good number of tests that check whether the function correctly identifies prime numbers. The tests also cover special cases such as 0, 1, and negative numbers.

Automatic unit test generation can be a useful way to get ideas for possible tests, but one should not expect the tests to be correct or the test suite to be comprehensive. It would be risky to assume that the automatically generated test suite is ready to use. In the example above, one problem is that the test suite does not include any tests with large numbers.

To get better results, we may instruct the AI on what tests it should create. By doing this, we can try to make sure that the test suite is comprehensive. Let's continue with the primality check example and ask the AI to generate tests that include all numbers between 0 and 100, negative numbers, and also large numbers.

> *Prompt*: I have created a Python function `is_prime(n)` that should check if the given number is prime. Can you create unit tests for the function?
>
> Test all inputs between 0 and 100 and present the tests in a compact form. Also test some negative numbers and some large numbers such as 999983 (prime) and 999997 (not prime).
>
> *Answer*: Below are the unit tests for the `is_prime(n)` function, covering various cases including numbers between 0 and 100, negative numbers, and some large numbers.
>
> ```python
> import unittest
>
> class TestIsPrime(unittest.TestCase):
>     def test_primes(self):
>         primes = [2, 3, 5, 7, 11, 13, 17, 19, 23, 29, 31, 37, 41,
>                   43, 47, 53, 59, 61, 67, 71, 73, 79, 83, 89, 97,
>                   999983]
>         for prime in primes:
>             self.assertTrue(is_prime(prime))
>
>     def test_non_primes(self):
>         non_primes = [0, 1, 4, 6, 8, 9, 10, 12, 14, 15, 16, 18,
>                       20, 21, 22, 24, 25, 26, 27, 28, 30, 32, 33,
>                       34, 35, 36, 38, 39, 40, 42, 44, 45, 46, 48,
>                       49, 50, 51, 52, 54, 55, 56, 57, 58, 60, 62,
>                       63, 64, 65, 66, 68, 69, 70, 72, 74, 75, 76,
>                       77, 78, 80, 81, 82, 84, 85, 86, 87, 88, 90,
>                       91, 92, 93, 94, 95, 96, 98, 99, 999997]
>         for non_prime in non_primes:
>             self.assertFalse(is_prime(non_prime))
>
>     def test_negative_numbers(self):
>         negative_numbers = [-1, -2, -3, -10, -100]
>         for negative in negative_numbers:
>             self.assertFalse(is_prime(negative))
>
> if __name__ == '__main__':
>     unittest.main()
> ```

The resulting test suite is comprehensive, and the tests are presented in a compact form as lists of numbers. Note that we specified that 999983 is prime and 999997 is not prime, because it could be difficult for AI to determine the primality of large numbers (see Sect. 8.1.2).

6.2.2 Password Validation

As another example, consider the task of creating unit tests for the JavaScript function `validPassword` discussed in Sect. 5.1.1. The function should check if a password contains at least 8 characters, both lowercase and uppercase letters, and at least one digit. In other words, there are four boolean features that must be true in a valid password:

- Feature 1: The length of the string is at least 8 characters.
- Feature 2: The string contains a lowercase character.
- Feature 3: The string contains an uppercase character.
- Feature 4: The string contains a digit.

A systematic way to test the function is to include a test for each possible combination of the features listed above. For example, to test a situation where features 2 and 4 are true, we could use the input string `test123`, which contains a lowercase letter and a digit, but is shorter than 8 characters and does not have an uppercase letter. Since there are four features, the total number of different combinations that should be tested is $2^4 = 16$.

Here is our first attempt to create the test suite:

Prompt: I have created a JavaScript function `validPassword` that should check if a password contains at least 8 characters, both lowercase and uppercase characters, and at least one digit. Can you create a test suite for the function?

Test all combinations of features (has length at least 8, contains lowercase, contains uppercase, contains digit) the input string can have.

Answer: Here's a test suite for the `validPassword` function in JavaScript, covering all combinations of the specified features:

```
const testCases = [
    // Feature 1: Length at least 8
    // Feature 2: Contains lowercase
    // Feature 3: Contains uppercase
    // Feature 4: Contains digit

    { password: "abcdefgh", expected: false }, // 2
    { password: "ABCDEFGH", expected: false }, // 3
    { password: "12345678", expected: false }, // 4
    { password: "abcdeFgh", expected: false }, // 1, 2, 3
    { password: "abcde123", expected: false }, // 1, 2, 4
    { password: "ABCDE123", expected: false }, // 1, 3, 4
    { password: "AbcdeFgh", expected: false }, // 1, 2, 3
    { password: "Abcde1gh", expected: true },  // 1, 2, 3, 4
    { password: "Abcdefg",  expected: false }, // 2, 3
    { password: "abcdefg1", expected: false }, // 2, 4
    { password: "ABCDEFG1", expected: false }, // 3, 4
```

6.2 Unit Test Generation

```
        { password: "abcdeF1g", expected: true },  // 1, 2, 3, 4
        { password: "1234567a", expected: false }, // 2, 4
        { password: "1234ABCD", expected: false }, // 3
        { password: "A1bcdefg", expected: true },  // 1, 2, 3, 4
];
```

Some tests in this test suite look good, but there are many issues. Some feature combinations are missing, and some are repeated. In several tests, the input has 8 characters, but feature 1 is marked as false. The input `1234ABCD` contains digits, but feature 4 is marked as false.

It seems that one major source of errors is correctly determining the length of the string. We can try to help the AI by describing the tests in a different way, dividing the tests into two groups based on the string length:

Prompt: I have created a JavaScript function `validPassword` that should check if a password contains at least 8 characters, both lowercase and uppercase characters, and at least one digit. Can you create a test suite for the function?

First test passwords where the length is at least 8. Test all combinations which character classes (lowercase, uppercase, digit) the password contains. After that, test passwords where the length is less than 8 in the same way.

Answer: Below is a JavaScript test suite for the `validPassword` function, covering all specified combinations of character classes based on the password length:

```
const testCases = [
    // Length >= 8
    { password: "Aa1aaaaa", expected: true },  // Lowercase,
    Uppercase, Digit
    { password: "aaaaaaaa", expected: false }, // Lowercase only
    { password: "aaaaaaa1", expected: false }, // Lowercase and
    Digit
    { password: "AAAAAAAA", expected: false }, // Uppercase only
    { password: "11111111", expected: false }, // Digit only
    { password: "AaAaAaAA", expected: false }, // Uppercase and
    Lowercase
    { password: "aaaaAAA1", expected: true },  // Lowercase,
    Uppercase, Digit
    { password: "A1A1A1A1", expected: true },  // Uppercase, Digit
    { password: "a1a1a1a1", expected: false }, // Lowercase, Digit

    // Length < 8
    { password: "Aa1", expected: false }, // Lowercase, Uppercase,
    Digit
    { password: "aaa", expected: false }, // Lowercase only
    { password: "aaa1", expected: false }, // Lowercase and Digit
    { password: "AAAA", expected: false }, // Uppercase only
    { password: "111", expected: false }, // Digit only
    { password: "AaA", expected: false }, // Uppercase and Lowercase
    { password: "aa1", expected: false }, // Lowercase, Digit
    { password: "A1", expected: false },  // Uppercase, Digit
];
```

This test suite looks somewhat better, but it still has issues. The input `A1A1A1A1` does not have any lowercase characters, but the expected result is true. There is no test where each feature is false. Once again, it is important that we carefully check the tests.

There are situations where using AI tools for test generation may not be a good choice, and the situation above is probably one of them. It would be more efficient to create the tests ourselves rather than spend time formulating different prompts and checking the results.

6.2.3 Evaluating Test Suites

Generating code that performs a well-specified task can be more straightforward than generating a test suite to test such code. While we can check that the generated tests run successfully, it can be difficult to know if the test suite is comprehensive. However, one thing we can do automatically is measure test coverage.

In a study [1], researchers used ChatGPT to generate tests for a set of Java methods from open source projects and examined the functionality and coverage of these tests. When evaluating test coverage, they focused on statement coverage, meaning how many lines of code are executed, and branch coverage, meaning how many branches in the code are covered.

Quite a few of the generated tests contained issues. Only 42% of the tests could be compiled without errors, and 25% of the tests could be executed successfully. If an error occurred during execution, it was usually because there was an incorrect assertion in the test code related to the code being tested. However, in the tests that worked, the statement and branch coverage were at the same level as in tests written by human programmers.

6.3 Extensive Testing

6.3.1 Regular Expression Testing

In Sect. 5.3.2, we considered the task of creating a regular expression that checks that the format of a given string is `YYYY-MM-DD` where `YYYY` denotes year, `MM` denotes month, and `DD` denotes day.

Creating such a regular expression is difficult for two reasons. First, the number of days in a month depends on the month. Second, the number of days in February depends on the year. The usual number of days in February is 28, but in leap years (such as 2024 and 2028) the number of days is 29.

6.3 Extensive Testing

Still, we can try to create such a regular expression for fun:[1]

Prompt: Generate a regular expression that checks that the given string has the format "YYYY-MM-DD". Please pay attention to the number of days in a month and leap years. You can assume that the year is between 1600 and 2400.

Answer: Creating a regular expression that accurately checks for the format "YYYY-MM-DD" while considering leap years and the number of days in each month is quite complex. Here's a regular expression that attempts to handle these details:

```
^(?:(?:(?:1[6-9]|2[0-3])\d{2})-(?:(?:0[13578]|1[02])-(?:0
[1-9]|[12]\d|3[01])|(?:0[469]|11)-(?:0[1-9]|[12]\d|30)|02
-(?:0[1-9]|1\d|2[0-8])))|(?:(?:1[6-9]|2[0-3])(?:0[48]|[24
68][048]|[13579][26])|1600|2000|2400)-02-29$
```

How do we know that the generated regular expression works correctly? Analyzing such a regular expression would be difficult, but we can thoroughly test how it works by comparing it to an alternative method for checking date strings. First let's create a function that checks the date string format *without* using a regular expression:

Prompt: Generate a Python function that checks if the given string has the date format "YYYY-MM-DD". Don't use regular expressions in the function.

Answer: Here's a function that utilizes the `datetime` module from the Python standard library to check if the given string is in the "YYYY-MM-DD" format and represents a valid date:

```python
from datetime import datetime

def is_valid_date_format(date_string):
    try:
        datetime.strptime(date_string, "%Y-%m-%d")
        return True
    except ValueError:
        return False
```

Next, we need comprehensive testing data. We can create the data as follows:

---

[1] Since the number of strings of the form YYYY-MM-DD is finite, we know that it is *possible* to create a regular expression to detect valid date strings. One method, which is not useful in practice, is to simply create a long expression of the form (1600-01-01|1600-01-02|...) that includes all valid dates. In fact, the real challenge here is how to create a relatively *short* regular expression for the task.

Prompt: Write Python code that creates a list of all possible strings of the form "YYYY-MM-DD" where YYYY is between 1600 and 2400, MM is between 01 and 12 and DD is between 00 and 31.

Answer: You can create a list of all possible strings in the format "YYYY-MM-DD" using Python's string formatting and list comprehensions. Below is a code snippet that accomplishes this:

```python
def generate_dates():
    dates = []
    for year in range(1600, 2401):   # Years from 1600 to 2400
        for month in range(1, 13):   # Months from 01 to 12
            for day in range(0, 32): # Days from 00 to 31
                # Format the date string
                date_str = f"{year:04d}-{month:02d}-{day:02d}"
                dates.append(date_str)
    return dates

# Call the function and store the result
date_list = generate_dates()
```

After that, we can create the following testing code that includes the regular expression we want to test and the above functions is_valid_date and generate_dates. The code iterates through all generated dates and compares the results of the regular expression and the function is_valid_date. If the two approaches yield a different result in some case, the code shows an error message.

```python
import re

regex = "^(?:(?:(?:1[6-9]|2[0-3])\d{2})-(?:(?:0[13578]|1[02])-(?:0
        [1-9]|[12]\d|3[01])|(?:0[469]|11)-(?:0[1-9]|[12]\d|30)|02
        -(?:0[1-9]|1\d|2[0-8])))|(?:(?:1[6-9]|2[0-3])(?:0[48]|[24
        68][048]|[13579][26])|1600|2000|2400)-02-29$"

date_list = generate_dates()

for date in date_list:
    result1 = is_valid_date_format(date)
    result2 = bool(re.match(regex, date))
    if result1 != result2:
        print("error:", date)
```

It turns out that the generated regular expression *almost* works. The code above tests the regular expression with about 300,000 cases, and it gives a wrong answer in only 365 tests where the year is 2400 and the day is not a leap day. The problem is that the year 2400 is only included in the special case that handles the leap day. Actually, we can easily fix the regular expression by replacing the part 2[0-3] with 2[0-4]. After this change, the testing code shows that the regular expression works correctly.

6.3.2 Verifying Algorithm Correctness

As another example on extensive testing, let's consider a stack sorting problem where the input list contains the numbers $1, 2, \ldots, n$ in some order. The task is to create a sorted output list using two stacks. On each step, we can either move the first number from the input list to the top of either stack, or move the top number from either stack to the end of the output list.

For example, the input list [1, 3, 4, 2] can be sorted as follows (Fig. 6.1):

1. Move the number 1 from the input list to the first stack.
2. Move the number 1 from the first stack to the output list.
3. Move the number 3 from the input list to the first stack.
4. Move the number 4 from the input list to the second stack.
5. Move the number 2 from the input list to the first stack.
6. Move the number 2 from the first stack to the output list.
7. Move the number 3 from the first stack to the output list.

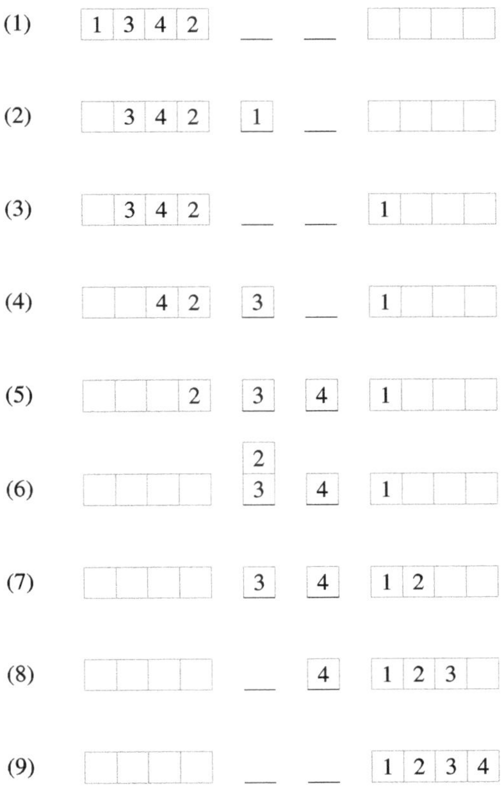

Fig. 6.1 Sorting the list [1, 3, 4, 2] using stack sorting

8. Move the number 4 from the second stack to the output list.

However, stack sorting is not always possible. For example, it is not possible to sort the list [2, 3, 4, 1]. After moving the number 2 to one of the stacks, the number 3 must be moved to the other stack, because it is not possible to collect the numbers from the stacks in the correct order if a larger number is on top of a smaller one. After this, however, the number 4 cannot be placed on either stack.

How can we find a sequence of moves that solves the problem? As mentioned above, we should never place a larger number on top of a smaller number. If there is only one possible stack for an input number, we should choose it. In addition, if a stack has the next number for the output list, we should always move it.

It turns out that the real challenge is how to choose a stack for an input number when both stacks are possible, i.e., they are empty or the top number is larger than the current number. Here is a possible greedy approach for this situation:

1. If both stacks are empty, choose either stack.
2. If one stack is empty, choose the stack that is not empty.
3. If no stack is empty, choose the stack whose top number is smaller.

The idea here is to make a move that restricts future moves as little as possible. For example, if the top numbers in the stacks are 3 and 5 and the next number is 2, the first stack is chosen after which the top numbers are 2 and 5. After that, we can still move the number 4 to the second stack, which would not be possible if we had moved the number 2 to it.

An algorithm using this approach seems to work in many situations. For the list [1, 3, 4, 2], it finds the solution presented above. For the list [2, 3, 4, 1], it does not find a solution, which is understandable because there is no solution. The algorithm also works for many other lists and the greedy idea seems reasonable. However, does the algorithm *always* find a solution if it is possible to sort the list?

There is a way to create an algorithm that certainly works using brute force: we can just go through all possible move sequences and check if any of them works. Then, using the brute force algorithm as a reference, we can extensively test our greedy algorithm. First, let's create Python implementations of the algorithms:

6.3 Extensive Testing

Prompt: The task is to sort a list that consists of numbers 1, 2, ..., *n* using two stacks. At the start, the input list contains the numbers to be sorted, and the output list is empty. The following operations are allowed:
- Move the first number from the input list to the top of either stack.
- Move the top number from either stack to the end of the output list.

Create a Python function `can_sort_brute` that returns true if the input list can be sorted and false otherwise. Create a brute force algorithm that goes through all possible move sequences.

Answer: Here is a brute-force algorithm in Python that tries all possible move sequences using recursion and backtracking. The function returns `True` if the input list can be sorted and `False` otherwise.

```
def can_sort_brute(input_list):
    # [...]
```

Prompt: Create a Python function `can_sort_greedy` that solves the same problem using a greedy algorithm. The function should move the number to a stack whose topmost number is larger than it. If there are two possible stacks, the stack with the smaller number is chosen. If there are no possible stacks, an empty stack is chosen. The function returns true if sorting is possible and false otherwise.

Answer: Here's the Python function implementing the described algorithm:

```
def can_sort_greedy(input_list):
    # [...]
```

The implemented functions work correctly in our two example cases, which is a good sign:

```
>>> can_sort_brute([1, 3, 4, 2])
True
>>> can_sort_brute([2, 3, 4, 1])
False
>>> can_sort_greedy([1, 3, 4, 2])
True
>>> can_sort_greedy([2, 3, 4, 1])
False
```

Next, let's create code for testing the functions using random inputs. If an input is found where the functions give different results, the input and the function return values are reported. We use small inputs (with list size between 1 and 8) for two reasons. First, the brute force algorithm would be too slow for larger lists. Second, if we find an input where the greedy algorithm fails, it will be convenient for us to analyze the input when the list is small.

Prompt: Write Python code that tests the two functions using random lists. In each test, the list consists of the numbers 1, 2, ..., n and n is between 1 and 8. If the functions give different results, stop testing and show the input where the results are different.

Answer: Here's a Python script that repeatedly generates random permutations of [1, 2, ..., n] for n between 1 and 8, and tests `can_sort_brute` and `can_sort_greedy` on them. If the results differ, it prints the problematic input and stops.

```
# [...]
def test_sort_functions(num_tests=10000):
    for _ in range(num_tests):
        n = random.randint(1, 8)
        lst = list(range(1, n+1))
        random.shuffle(lst)
        result_brute = can_sort_brute(lst)
        result_greedy = can_sort_greedy(lst)
        if result_brute != result_greedy:
            print(f"Discrepancy found for input: {lst}")
            print(f"can_sort_brute: {result_brute}")
            print(f"can_sort_greedy: {result_greedy}")
            return
    print("All tests passed. No discrepancies found.")
```

After running the testing code for some time, we actually find an input where the greedy algorithm gives a wrong answer:

```
Discrepancy found for input: [6, 2, 4, 1, 7, 3, 5]
can_sort_brute: True
can_sort_greedy: False
```

In this case the greedy algorithm moves the numbers 6 and 2 to the first stack, the number 4 to the second stack, and the number 1 to the first stack. Then the numbers 1 and 2 are moved to the output list. Now it is not possible to move the number 7 to any stack because the top numbers in the stacks are 6 and 4. However, using another approach, we move the numbers 6 and 4 to the first stack and the numbers 2 and 1 to the second stack. Then, after moving the numbers 1 and 2 to the output list, the second stack is empty and we can move the number 7 to it and also process the rest of the input list. This example shows that the greedy algorithm is *not* correct.[2]

Now that we know that the greedy algorithm does not work, we can also find the smallest example where it does not work:

---

[2] This was a surprise to me some years ago when I used this problem in my data structures and algorithms course. The greedy algorithm seemed intuitively correct to me and I "proved" that it works, but then a student showed me an example where it does not work.

6.4 User Interface Testing

> *Prompt*: Modify the testing function so that instead of generating random tests, it goes through all lists from shortest to longest up to a maximum length of $n = 8$ and finds the first list where the greedy algorithm doesn't work.
>
> *Answer*: To systematically test all possible permutations of [1, 2, ..., n] for n from 1 to 8, you can use `itertools.permutations`. The function below will go through all such permutations (from shortest to longest) and report the first input where `can_sort_brute` and `can_sort_greedy` give different results.
>
> ```
> # [...]
> def test_sort_functions_exhaustive(max_n=8):
>     for n in range(1, max_n+1):
>         base_list = list(range(1, n+1))
>         for perm in itertools.permutations(base_list):
>             lst = list(perm)
>             result_brute = can_sort_brute(lst)
>             result_greedy = can_sort_greedy(lst)
>             if result_brute != result_greedy:
>                 print(f"Discrepancy found for input: {lst}")
>                 print(f"can_sort_brute: {result_brute}")
>                 print(f"can_sort_greedy: {result_greedy}")
>                 return
>     print("All tests passed. No discrepancies found.")
> ```

It turns out that the smallest list is as follows:

```
Discrepancy found for input: [5, 2, 4, 1, 6, 3]
can_sort_brute: True
can_sort_greedy: False
```

Thus, the greedy algorithm works correctly when the list has at most five numbers, but it doesn't always work correctly for larger lists.[3]

The testing technique discussed above is often useful when we have implemented a complex algorithm and want to check whether the implementation works correctly. AI tools are good at creating brute force algorithms and writing code for comparing different algorithm implementations.

6.4 User Interface Testing

As the final topic in this chapter, let's create user interface tests for a web application. We would like to automatically test a simple web application where a user can read existing messages and send a new message. The testing code should simulate how the application is used in a web browser. What would be a good library for that?

---

[3] While the greedy algorithm doesn't work, there are efficient algorithms for solving the problem. Creating such an algorithm is a good algorithm design challenge.

Fig. 6.2 Step 1: Click "Send message"

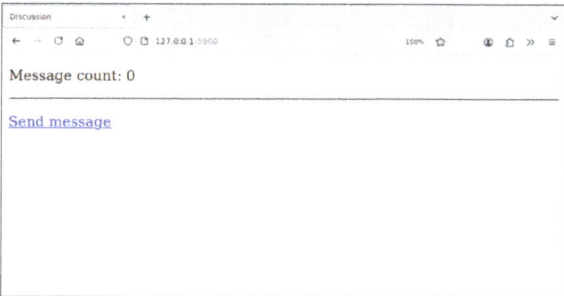

Fig. 6.3 Step 2: Write a message and send it

> *Prompt*: I would like to create automated tests for a web application. The test program should be written in Python and use the application in a browser like a real user. What would be a good library for that?
>
> *Answer*: For creating automated tests that interact with a web application in a browser like a real user, Selenium WebDriver is an excellent choice. Selenium allows you to automate browser actions such as clicking, inputting text, and navigating through your application, mimicking how an actual user would interact with it.

Let's try to use Selenium. Figures 6.2, 6.3 and 6.4 show the steps the test code should take. First, the test user should click a link to send a new message, then write the message and click the button, and finally check that the new message can be seen in the list of messages.

We can try to create the testing program as follows:

Fig. 6.4 Step 3: Check that you can see the message

Prompt: Create a Selenium test for a web application. The test should do as follows:
- Go to index page, click on the link "Send message".
- Fill in a test message to the textarea, click the submit button.
- Check that you are back at the index page and see the message you posted.

Answer: Here's an example of how you can write this test using Python's `unittest` framework and Selenium.

```
import unittest
from selenium import webdriver
from selenium.webdriver.common.keys import Keys
from selenium.webdriver.common.by import By
from selenium.webdriver.support.ui import WebDriverWait
from selenium.webdriver.support import expected_conditions as EC

class FlaskAppTestCase(unittest.TestCase):

    def setUp(self):
        # Setup the Chrome WebDriver
        self.driver = webdriver.Chrome()
        self.driver.get("http://localhost:5000")  # Adjust the URL to where your app is hosted

    def test_message_posting(self):
        driver = self.driver

        # Step 1: Click on the link "Send message"
        send_message_link = driver.find_element(By.LINK_TEXT, "Send message")
        send_message_link.click()

        # Wait for the textarea to be visible
        WebDriverWait(driver, 10).until(
            EC.visibility_of_element_located((By.NAME, "message"))
        )

        # Step 2: Fill in a test message to the textarea and submit
        message_textarea = driver.find_element(By.NAME, "message")
        message_textarea.send_keys("This is a test message")
        submit_button = driver.find_element(By.CSS_SELECTOR, "input[type='submit']")
        submit_button.click()

        # Wait to be redirected back to the index page
        WebDriverWait(driver, 10).until(
            EC.visibility_of_element_located((By.TAG_NAME, "body"))
```

```
            )
            # Step 3: Verify the posted message appears on the index
        page
            body_text = driver.find_element(By.TAG_NAME, "body").text
            self.assertIn("This is a test message", body_text)

    def tearDown(self):
        self.driver.close()

if __name__ == "__main__":
    unittest.main()
```

The testing program already looks quite good. It assumes that the application can be found at `http://localhost:5000`, which is the default address for web applications created using the Flask library in Python. As we requested, the program tries to click the link, send a message, and check that it can see the message.

However, the program does not work at the moment because it assumes that the name of the textarea is `message`. This is not true, and the program cannot locate the textarea. Let's try to fix the problem as follows:

Prompt: Do not assume that form elements have specific names. Can you update the code?

Answer: If we can't rely on specific names for form elements, we have to resort to other attributes or relative positioning to locate elements. Here's how you can update the Selenium test to handle such scenarios:

```
        [...]
        # Step 2: Fill in a test message to the textarea and submit
        message_textarea = driver.find_element(By.TAG_NAME, "textarea")
        message_textarea.send_keys("This is a test message")

        [...]
```

Now the program finds a `textarea` element and does not assume that the element has a specific name. After this change, the program works and shows that the test is successful.

Since our web application displays simple HTML pages, the `WebDriverWait` parts in the code may not actually be necessary. We can simplify the program by removing those parts and comments:

Prompt: Can you remove the `WebDriverWait` parts from the code (and their imports)? I think they are not necessary. Can you also remove the comments?

Answer: If you believe that explicit waits (`WebDriverWait`) are not necessary due to either the simplicity of your application or because it loads quickly enough, you can simplify the Selenium test by removing those waits. Here's the updated test code without `WebDriverWait` and comments:

```python
import unittest
from selenium import webdriver
from selenium.webdriver.common.by import By

class FlaskAppTestCase(unittest.TestCase):

    def setUp(self):
        self.driver = webdriver.Chrome()
        self.driver.get("http://localhost:5000")

    def test_message_posting(self):
        driver = self.driver
        send_message_link = driver.find_element(By.PARTIAL_LINK_TEXT, "Send message")
        send_message_link.click()
        message_textarea = driver.find_element(By.TAG_NAME, "textarea")
        message_textarea.send_keys("This is a test message")
        submit_button = driver.find_element(By.CSS_SELECTOR, "input[type='submit']")
        submit_button.click()
        body_text = driver.find_element(By.TAG_NAME, "body").text
        self.assertIn("This is a test message", body_text)

    def tearDown(self):
        self.driver.close()

if __name__ == "__main__":
    unittest.main()
```

Reference

1. Z. Yuan, M. Liu, S. Ding, et al., Evaluating and improving ChatGPT for unit test generation. Proc. ACM Softw. Eng. **1**(FSE), 1703–1726 (2024)

Code Analysis

7

This chapter discusses topics related to using AI tools in code analysis: explaining code, generating code reviews, formatting and refactoring code, and converting code from one programming language to another.

Section 7.1 presents examples of how AI tools can be used to explain code. When given complex code without context, we can often automatically get a comprehensive description that explains the purpose and functioning of the code.

Section 7.2 discusses creating code reviews using AI tools, which can provide useful feedback about our code. However, it is not always advisable to apply AI-generated suggestions; it is the programmer's responsibility to decide which changes are worth making.

Section 7.3 demonstrates how AI tools can be used for formatting and refactoring code. Compared to traditional tools for these tasks, AI tools offer more possibilities because they have a deeper understanding of the code and its context.

Section 7.4 focuses on automatically converting code from one programming language to another. The challenge here is that some concepts exist only in certain languages, such as static types in variables.

7.1 Explaining Code

A task very suitable for AI tools is to explain what a given piece of code does. AI tools are often able to understand code surprisingly well, even without extra information about what the code is supposed to do. The following examples provide samples of AI's ability to explain code.

7.1.1 Lisp Expressions

Let's look at the following Python function that calculates the value of a Lisp-style arithmetic expression. The idea is that inside the parentheses, there is first an operator, either + or *, followed by expressions that should be added or multiplied together. For example, the value of the expression (+ 2 3) is 5, and the value of the expression (* (+ 2 3) (+ 1 1 1)) is 15.

Prompt: What does the following Python function do?

```
from functools import reduce

def calc(e):
    rpos = e.index(")")
    if rpos == len(e) - 1:
        e = e[1:-1].split(" ")
        values = [int(v) for v in e[1:]]
        if e[0] == "+":
            return reduce(lambda x, y: x + y, values, 0)
        if e[0] == "*":
            return reduce(lambda x, y: x * y, values, 1)
    lpos = e.rindex("(", 0, rpos)
    return calc(e[:lpos] + str(calc(s[lpos:rpos+1])) + s[rpos+1:])
```

Answer: The provided Python function calc is a simple expression evaluator for a specific type of arithmetic expression that uses a prefix notation with parentheses. Let's break down what it does:

1. Identify the Right Parenthesis (): The function finds the position of the first closing parenthesis using rpos = e.index(")").
2. Check if the Closing Parenthesis is at the End: It checks if this closing parenthesis is at the end of the string e. If true, it indicates that the expression is fully enclosed in parentheses.
3. Evaluate the Expression within Parentheses:

   - It removes the outer parentheses and splits the expression by spaces to separate the operator and operands: e = e[1:-1].split(" ").
   - The first element e[0] is the operator, which can be either + for addition or * for multiplication.
   - The subsequent elements are the operands, which are converted to integers: values = [int(v) for v in e[1:]].

4. Perform the Operation:

   - If the operator is "+", it uses reduce to sum all the operands: reduce(lambda x, y: x + y, values, 0).
   - If the operator is "*", it uses reduce to multiply all the operands: reduce(lambda x, y: x * y, values, 1).

7.1 Explaining Code

5. Recurse for Nested Expressions:

   - If the closing parenthesis is not at the end, the function finds the last opening parenthesis before the closing parenthesis: `lpos = e.rindex("(", 0, rpos)`.
   - It recursively evaluates the innermost expression and replaces it in the original string, continuing until the entire expression is evaluated.

Example Usage:

- `calc("(+ 1 2 3)")` would return 6, as it evaluates the sum of 1, 2, and 3.
- `calc("(* 2 3 4)")` would return 24, as it evaluates the product of 2, 3, and 4.
- For nested expressions like `calc("(+ 1 (* 2 3))")`, it first evaluates `(* 2 3)` to 6, and then `(+ 1 6)` to 7.

The function does not handle errors or invalid input gracefully,
so it assumes that the input is always correctly formatted according to the expected pattern.

7.1.2 Assembly Code

As another example, assume we have some x86 assembly code that we would like to analyze. Explaining such a piece of code without any prior knowledge of its functionality would be a difficult task even for an experienced human programmer.

Prompt: Give a brief summary of the following assembly code:

```
0000000000401000 <_start>:
  401000:   b8 01 00 00 00        mov    $0x1,%eax
  401005:   bf 01 00 00 00        mov    $0x1,%edi
  40100a:   48 8d 74 24 ff        lea    -0x1(%rsp),%rsi
  40100f:   ba 01 00 00 00        mov    $0x1,%edx
  401014:   b3 08                 mov    $0x8,%bl

0000000000401016 <row>:
  401016:   b7 08                 mov    $0x8,%bh
  401018:   c6 44 24 ff 30        movb   $0x30,-0x1(%rsp)
  40101d:   88 dd                 mov    %bl,%ch
  40101f:   80 e5 01              and    $0x1,%ch
  401022:   30 6c 24 ff           xor    %ch,-0x1(%rsp)

0000000000401026 <col>:
  401026:   80 74 24 ff 01        xorb   $0x1,-0x1(%rsp)
  40102b:   0f 05                 syscall
  40102d:   fe cf                 dec    %bh
  40102f:   80 ff 00              cmp    $0x0,%bh
  401032:   75 f2                 jne    401026 <col>
  401034:   c6 44 24 ff 0a        movb   $0xa,-0x1(%rsp)
  401039:   0f 05                 syscall
  40103b:   fe cb                 dec    %bl
  40103d:   80 fb 00              cmp    $0x0,%bl
  401040:   75 d4                 jne    401016 <row>
  401042:   b8 3c 00 00 00        mov    $0x3c,%eax
  401047:   bf 00 00 00 00        mov    $0x0,%edi
  40104c:   0f 05                 syscall
```

Answer: This assembly code prints an 8x8 checkerboard pattern of alternating '0's and '1's (like a chessboard) to the terminal, using Linux system calls, and then exits. Each row alternates starting with '0' or '1', producing output like:

```
01010101
10101010
01010101
10101010
01010101
10101010
01010101
10101010
```

Prompt: Great work! Can you now explain each instruction in the code?

Answer: Here is your code, commented line by line to clarify what each instruction does.

```
mov     $0x1,%eax           # syscall number for sys_write (1)
mov     $0x1,%edi           # file descriptor: 1 (stdout)
lea     -0x1(%rsp),%rsi     # pointer to buffer at (%rsp - 1)
mov     $0x1,%edx           # number of bytes to write (1)
mov     $0x8,%bl            # outer loop counter (rows), bl = 8

mov     $0x8,%bh            # inner loop counter (columns), bh = 8
movb    $0x30,-0x1(%rsp)    # store ASCII '0' in buffer at (%rsp - 1)
mov     %bl,%ch             # copy row counter (bl) into ch
and     $0x1,%ch            # ch = bl & 1 (row parity: even/odd)
xor     %ch,-0x1(%rsp)      # XOR buffer byte with row parity

xorb    $0x1,-0x1(%rsp)     # XOR buffer byte with 1
syscall                     # write the byte (either '0' or '1')
dec     %bh                 # decrement column counter
cmp     $0x0,%bh            # columns done?
jne     401026 <col>        # if not, repeat inner loop

movb    $0xa,-0x1(%rsp)     # store ASCII newline '\n' in buffer
syscall                     # write the newline
dec     %bl                 # decrement row counter
cmp     $0x0,%bl            # rows done?
jne     401016 <row>        # if not, repeat outer loop

mov     $0x3c,%eax          # syscall number for sys_exit (60)
mov     $0x0,%edi           # exit code 0
syscall                     # exit
```

7.2 Code Review

AI tools can be used to help review code by asking them for feedback and suggestions on how to improve the code. The suggestions from AI can be useful, but as always, the programmer is responsible for the code. In the following example, we use AI to review a Python class.

7.2.1 Review Round 1

Consider a class called `SpellChecker` that implements a simple spell checker in Python. The constructor of the class takes a file that contains a list of words, and the `check` method goes through each word in a given string and returns the words that are not in the list. Let's generate a review for the code:

Prompt: Review the following code. First, provide a list of suggestions on how the code could be improved. After that, show the revised code.

```
class SpellChecker:
    def __init__(self, file):
        self.words = set()
        for line in open(file).readlines():
            self.words.add(line.strip())

    def check(self, text):
        words = text.split(" ")
        results = []

        for word in words:
            modified_word = word.lower()
            if modified_word[-1] in ".,!?;":
                modified_word = modified_word[:-1]
            if modified_word not in self.words:
                results.append(word)

        return results
```

Answer: Suggestions for Improvement:

1. File Handling: Use a context manager (`with` statement) when opening files to ensure they are properly closed.
2. Performance: Avoid calling `open(file).readlines()` in a loop; instead, use `with open(file) as f` and iterate directly over the file.
3. Word Normalization: Handle punctuation more robustly (e.g., words surrounded by quotes, parentheses, or multiple punctuation marks).
4. Lowercasing: Store all dictionary words in lowercase for consistent comparison.
5. Splitting Words: Use `text.split()` instead of `text.split(" ")` to handle multiple spaces and tabs.
6. Punctuation Handling: Use `str.strip()` with a set of punctuation characters to clean words.
7. Efficiency: Predefine the set of punctuation characters to strip.
8. Variable Naming: Use more descriptive variable names where appropriate.
9. Error Handling: Optionally, handle the case where the file does not exist or is unreadable.
10. Code Readability: Improve spacing and structure for better readability.

Revised Code:

```
import string

class SpellChecker:
    def __init__(self, filename):
        self.words = set()
        try:
            with open(filename) as f:
```

```
                for line in f:
                    word = line.strip().lower()
                    if word:
                        self.words.add(word)
        except IOError:
            print("Error: Could not open the dictionary file.")

        self.punctuation = set(string.punctuation)

    def check(self, text):
        words_in_text = text.split()
        misspelled = []

        for word in words_in_text:
            cleaned_word = word.lower().strip(string.punctuation)
            if cleaned_word and cleaned_word not in self.words:
                misspelled.append(word)

        return misspelled
```

The review highlights some shortcomings in the code related to file handling. Using a context manager and adding error handling are good suggestions that improve code quality. It is less clear whether the suggested way to go through the file lines actually makes a real difference in terms of efficiency.

The review also suggests changes related to how words and punctuation are handled. These changes would affect how the code works, and the challenge here is that it has not been clearly specified how the code should behave in different situations. In this case, the programmer should think carefully about what they actually want to achieve, instead of just accepting the AI's suggestions as they are.

7.2.2 Review Round 2

Earlier, in the context of testing code, we noticed that if we ask AI to find a bug in code, it may even invent a bug just to find something. The same risk exists when reviewing code, because AI tends to always suggest something to change. As a test, let's make a review for the code that the AI just revised:

> *Prompt*: Review the following code. First provide a list of suggestions on how the code could be improved. After that, show the revised code.

```
import string

class SpellChecker:
    def __init__(self, filename):
        self.words = set()
        try:
            with open(filename) as f:
                for line in f:
                    word = line.strip().lower()
                    if word:
                        self.words.add(word)
        except IOError:
            print("Error: Could not open the dictionary file.")
```

7.2 Code Review

```
            self.punctuation = set(string.punctuation)

    def check(self, text):
        words_in_text = text.split()
        misspelled = []

        for word in words_in_text:
            cleaned_word = word.lower().strip(string.punctuation)
            if cleaned_word and cleaned_word not in self.words:
                misspelled.append(word)

        return misspelled
```

Answer: Suggestions for Improvement:

1. Error Handling: Instead of printing an error and continuing, the constructor should raise an exception if the dictionary file can't be opened. This allows users of the class to handle errors more appropriately.
2. Punctuation Cleaning: The current method only strips punctuation from the beginning and end of words, missing internal punctuation (e.g., `don't` becomes `dont`). Consider using regular expressions to remove all punctuation or handle contractions more intelligently.
3. Case Sensitivity: The code lowercases dictionary words and input words, which is good. However, the `misspelled` list returns the original word, which may be inconsistent for further processing. Consider returning the cleaned word or both the original and cleaned versions.
4. Efficiency: Storing `self.punctuation` is unnecessary since `string.punctuation` is only used in one place. Remove this attribute if not needed elsewhere.
5. File Encoding: Specify the file encoding (e.g., UTF-8) when opening files to avoid platform-dependent issues.
6. Code Readability: Improve readability by separating concerns and adding comments where necessary.
7. Edge Cases: The code does not handle empty input text or an empty dictionary gracefully. Add appropriate checks or document this behavior.
8. Resource Management: Using `with` when opening files is good practice and is already implemented.

Revised Code:

```
import string
import re

class SpellChecker:
    def __init__(self, filename):
        self.words = set()
        try:
            with open(filename, encoding='utf-8') as f:
                for line in f:
                    word = line.strip().lower()
                    if word:
                        self.words.add(word)
        except IOError as e:
            raise RuntimeError("Could not open the dictionary file: " + str(e))

    def check(self, text):
```

```
            # Use regex to extract words, ignoring punctuation
            words_in_text = re.findall(r'\b\w+\b', text.lower())
            misspelled = []

            for word in words_in_text:
                if word and word not in self.words:
                    misspelled.append(word)

            return misspelled
```

The revised code after the second review round includes better file error handling, specifies the encoding when opening the file, and uses a more complex method to remove punctuation with a regular expression. Interestingly, the first review suggested creating the variable `self.punctuation` to store the punctuation characters, while the second review recommended removing this variable.

This is where the programmer's expertise becomes important: not all suggestions in code reviews are helpful or improve the code. The more review rounds we have, the more suggestions we get, and the code usually becomes more complex after each round. Therefore, we should understand which changes are relevant and when it is time to stop asking for new suggestions.

In this example, there is a clear difference between the two review rounds. The feedback in the first round can clearly help improve the quality of the code. In contrast, the feedback in the second round feels somewhat artificial.

7.3 Code Formatting and Refactoring

With the help of AI tools, it is possible to do many kinds of code formatting and refactoring that have traditionally required special tools. For example, we can ask AI to make sure that the code style follows Python's conventions, or to change a variable's name in all the places where it appears.

However, using AI is often not a good idea in these situations. For simple tasks, traditional established tools tend to be more efficient and reliable. If we want to check Python programming style, there are good linters for this purpose. If we want to change a variable's name, programming editors have good features for that.

Still, AI can be useful when the task we want to perform is so complex that traditional tools cannot handle it. Typically, before AI tools, such tasks would have required the work of a human programmer.

7.3.1 Improving Names

Let's look at an example where we have existing Python code with variable and function names that are not easy to understand and do not follow the usual Python conventions. We can improve the code using the following prompt:

7.3 Code Formatting and Refactoring

Prompt: Improve the names in the following code:

```python
def calc(numberList):
    cnt = 0
    for x in numberList:
        if x % 2 == 0:
            cnt += 1
    return cnt
```

Answer: To improve the readability and clarity of the code, we can rename the function and its parameters to better describe their purpose. Here's a revised version:

```python
def count_even_numbers(numbers):
    even_count = 0
    for number in numbers:
        if number % 2 == 0:
            even_count += 1
    return even_count
```

In the revised code, the names are descriptive and follow Python conventions. Even though the function is simple, choosing good names required understanding what the code does. For example, the new function name `count_even_numbers` clearly describes what the function does.

7.3.2 Removing Repetition

In the following example, our code has two parts with the same structure. In both parts, we calculate the median of a list of numbers. We can improve the code by creating a function for calculating the median:

Prompt: Can you remove repetition from the following code?

```python
sorted_dataset = sorted(first_dataset)
count = len(sorted_dataset)
median = sorted_dataset[count // 2]
print("Median in first dataset:", median)

sorted_dataset = sorted(second_dataset)
count = len(sorted_dataset)
median = sorted_dataset[count // 2]
print("Median in second dataset:", median)
```

Answer: You can remove the repetition in your code by creating a function that calculates the median for any given dataset. Here's a refactored version of your code:

Fig. 7.1 A path from the upper-left corner to the lower-right corner in a 5 × 5 grid

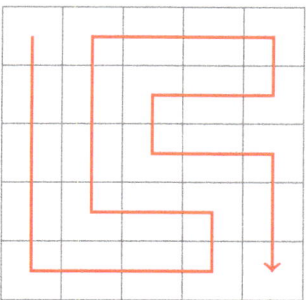

```python
def calculate_median(dataset):
    sorted_dataset = sorted(dataset)
    count = len(sorted_dataset)
    return sorted_dataset[count // 2]

first_median = calculate_median(first_dataset)
print("Median in first dataset:", first_median)

second_median = calculate_median(second_dataset)
print("Median in second dataset:", second_median)
```

7.3.3 Advanced Refactoring

As an example of more advanced refactoring, let's look at the following C++ function that uses a backtracking algorithm to calculate the number of grid paths from the upper-left corner to the lower-right corner. For example, when $N = 5$, the total number of such paths is 104. Figure 7.1 shows one possible path in this situation.

The current code is repetitive because, at each step, the path can go in four directions, and there is a separate if block for each direction. First, let's see what happens if we try to improve the code without specifying exactly what should be changed:

Prompt: I have the following C++ code that counts the number of paths in a grid. Can you make the code more compact and easier to understand?

```cpp
const int N = 5;

bool visited[N][N];
int total_count;

void search(int y, int x, int count) {
    if (y == N - 1 && x == N - 1 && count == N * N) {
        total_count++;
        return;
    }

    if (y + 1 < N && !visited[y + 1][x]) {
```

7.3 Code Formatting and Refactoring

```
            visited[y + 1][x] = true;
            search(y + 1, x, count + 1);
            visited[y + 1][x] = false;
        }

        if (y - 1 >= 0 && !visited[y - 1][x]) {
            visited[y - 1][x] = true;
            search(y - 1, x, count + 1);
            visited[y - 1][x] = false;
        }

        if (x + 1 < N && !visited[y][x + 1]) {
            visited[y][x + 1] = true;
            search(y, x + 1, count + 1);
            visited[y][x + 1] = false;
        }

        if (x - 1 >= 0 && !visited[y][x - 1]) {
            visited[y][x - 1] = true;
            search(y, x - 1, count + 1);
            visited[y][x - 1] = false;
        }
    }
```

Answer: You can make the given C++ code more compact and elegant by reducing redundancy and using a more systematic approach for exploring the neighboring cells. Here's a revised version of your code:

```
const int N = 5;

bool visited[N][N];
int total_count;

void search(int y, int x, int count) {
    if (y == N - 1 && x == N - 1 && count == N * N) {
        total_count++;
        return;
    }

    // Down, Up, Right, Left
    int directions[4][2] = {{1, 0}, {-1, 0}, {0, 1}, {0, -1}};

    for (auto& dir : directions) {
        int newY = y + dir[0], newX = x + dir[1];
        if (newY >= 0 && newY < N && newX >= 0 && newX < N && !visited[newY][newX]) {
            visited[newY][newX] = true;
            search(newY, newX, count + 1);
            visited[newY][newX] = false;
        }
    }
}
```

This is a good way to improve the code: instead of four separate if blocks, the code uses a for loop that does the same thing for each direction. However, we can make the code even shorter and easier to understand by using a more detailed prompt that suggests adding a new check at the beginning of the function:

Prompt: I have the following C++ code that counts the number of paths in a grid. Can you modify the function so that the boundary and visited checks only happen at the beginning of the function?

```
[...]
```

Answer: To modify the function so that the boundary and visited checks only happen at the beginning, we can first check if the current position is valid and mark it as visited. If it is not valid, we can return immediately. This way, we only need to perform the checks once, and the recursive calls can proceed without additional checks for each direction. Here's the revised code:

```cpp
const int N = 5;

bool visited[N][N];
int total_count;

void search(int y, int x, int count) {
    if (y < 0 || y >= N || x < 0 || x >= N || visited[y][x]) {
        return;
    }

    if (y == N - 1 && x == N - 1 && count == N * N) {
        total_count++;
        return;
    }

    visited[y][x] = true;

    search(y + 1, x, count + 1); // Down
    search(y - 1, x, count + 1); // Up
    search(y, x + 1, count + 1); // Right
    search(y, x - 1, count + 1); // Left

    visited[y][x] = false;
}
```

7.4 Code Conversion

Another use case for automatic code analysis is converting code from one language to another. This can be useful, for example, when a new version of an application is being developed in a different language, or when the same code needs to run in both the backend and frontend, which use different languages.

7.4.1 Simple Examples

Let's start with an example where we convert a function from PHP to JavaScript. The conversion is simple because each line in the original function can be directly replaced by a corresponding line in the new function.

Prompt: Here is a PHP function that checks if the format of a username is valid. Please create a JavaScript version of that function.

```
function valid_username($username) {
    if (strlen($username) < 1 || strlen($username) > 16) {
        return false;
    }

    for ($i = 0; $i < strlen($username); $i++) {
        $code = ord($username[$i]);
        if ($code <= 32 || $code > 127) {
            return false;
        }
    }

    return true;
}
```

Answer: Here's a JavaScript version of the `valid_username` function that performs the same checks for the validity of a username:

```
function validUsername(username) {
    if (username.length < 1 || username.length > 16) {
        return false;
    }

    for (let i = 0; i < username.length; i++) {
        const code = username.charCodeAt(i);
        if (code <= 32 || code > 127) {
            return false;
        }
    }

    return true;
}
```

Next, let's convert code from Python to C. The original Python code uses the `count` method to find out how many times the letter "e" appears in a string. There is no such function in the C standard library, so the converted code counts the occurrences using a for loop.

Prompt: How can I write the following Python code in C?

```
text = "The quick brown fox jumps over the lazy dog"
print(text.count("e"))
```

Answer: To convert the given Python code into C, you will need to use C's string handling functions. The Python code counts the occurrences of the letter "e" in the string. In C, you can achieve this using a simple loop to iterate through the string and count the occurrences.

```c
const char *text = "The quick brown fox jumps over the lazy dog";
char target = 'e';
int count = 0;

// Iterate through each character in the string
for (int i = 0; text[i] != '\0'; i++) {
    if (text[i] == target) {
        count++;
    }
}

// Print the count of 'e'
printf("%d\n", count);
```

Note that the AI "changed its mind" while generating the answer. The first sentence says that C's string handling functions should be used, but the actual implementation uses a for loop instead of string functions.

7.4.2 Conversion Accuracy

One difficulty in converting between programming languages is that in some languages, the type of every variable is written in the code, but in other languages, it is not. For example, let's look at the following situation where we want to convert a median function from Python to Java:

Prompt: Can you convert the following Python function to Java?

```python
def median(numbers):
    numbers = sorted(numbers)
    return numbers[len(numbers) // 2]
```

Answer: Below is the equivalent Java function for the given Python function:

```java
public static int median(int[] numbers) {
    Arrays.sort(numbers);
    return numbers[numbers.length / 2];
}
```

Here, the challenge is that the Python code does not tell us the type of `numbers`. Can we assume that `numbers` is a list? Are the numbers integers or floats? How large can the numbers be? We would need more context to convert the function accurately. In the conversion above, it is assumed that the numbers are integers and small enough to fit in the 32-bit `int` type in Java.

7.4 Code Conversion

Note that there is also an important difference between the original and the converted code. In Python, the `sorted` function creates a new sorted list and does not sort the original list. However, the `Arrays.sort` method used in the Java code sorts the original list. In practice, the difference can be shown like this:

```
numbers = [3, 2, 1]
print(median(numbers)) # 2
print(numbers[0]) # 3
```

```
int[] numbers = {3, 2, 1};
System.out.println(median(numbers)); // 2
System.out.println(numbers[0]); // 1
```

In the Python code, the first element of the list `numbers` does not change when the `median` function is called. In the Java code, however, the first element of the array `numbers` changes when the `median` method is called. Again, it is very important to check AI-generated code before using it.

Sometimes the differences between languages can be subtle. In the following example, one could first think that the conversion is accurate:

Prompt: Convert the following Python function to Java:

```
def fix_hour(hour):
    return hour % 12
```

Answer: Below is the equivalent Java function for the given Python function:

```
public static int fixHour(int hour) {
    return hour % 12;
}
```

As in the previous example, the type of the parameter `hour` is not specified, and the converted code assumes that the `int` type can be used. However, even if we ignore the parameter type, the Java method is *not* equivalent to the Python function. The following code shows the difference:

```
print(fix_hour(-1)) # 11
```

```
System.out.println(fixHour(-1)); // -1
```

In Python, the result of the remainder operator `%` is always a nonnegative number, which is actually surprising because the convention in most programming languages (including Java) is that the result of the remainder operator can be a negative number. Let's try to fix the issue:

Prompt: The Java % operator differs from the Python % operator. Can you fix the converted function so that it works correctly?

Answer: In Java, the % operator behaves the same as in Python for positive numbers but can differ for negative numbers. To ensure consistent behavior between Python and Java, especially when dealing with negative numbers, we can adjust the calculation to handle negative values properly. Here's the corrected Java function:

```java
public static int fixHour(int hour) {
    int result = hour % 12;
    return result < 0 ? result + 12 : result;
}
```

With this fix, the function works correctly. If the result of the remainder operation is negative, the number 12 is added to the result.

7.4.3 Style Differences

Another difficulty in converting code is that different languages have different characteristic ways to express things. In the following example, we convert a list processing function from Haskell to Python. The function counts the number of even numbers in a given list.

Prompt: Convert the following Haskell function to Python:

```haskell
countEvens :: [Int] -> Int
countEvens [] = 0
countEvens (x:xs)
    | even x    = 1 + countEvens xs
    | otherwise = countEvens xs
```

Answer: Here's the equivalent Python function:

```python
def count_evens(lst):
    if not lst:
        return 0
    else:
        x, xs = lst[0], lst[1:]
        if x % 2 == 0:
            return 1 + count_evens(xs)
        else:
            return count_evens(xs)
```

Haskell is a functional programming language where it is natural to use recursion to process a list. The Haskell function above uses pattern matching: the result for the empty list [ ] is 0, and otherwise the result is calculated recursively. The syntax

7.4 Code Conversion

(x:xs) means that the list is divided into two parts: x is the first element and xs denotes the rest of the list. If x is even, the result is increased by one.

The Python function above is directly converted from the Haskell function. In this situation, it is possible but not typical to use recursion in Python. In practice, using the Python function would be difficult because the default recursion stack size in Python is small, and it would not be possible to process large lists. In Haskell, there is no such problem because tail recursion elimination is used automatically.

We can create a more *Pythonic* function, i.e. a function that uses a programming style characteristic to Python, as follows:

Prompt: Can you create a more Pythonic version of the function?

Answer: A more Pythonic way to implement this function would be to use list comprehensions and the sum function:

```
def count_evens(lst):
    return sum(1 for x in lst if x % 2 == 0)
```

This function is completely different from the Haskell function. The number of even numbers is counted using the sum function and a generator expression, which goes through the list and checks which elements are even numbers. The value 1 means that the sum increases by one for each such element.

Limitations of AI Tools

8

This chapter discusses the limitations of AI tools, with a focus on programming-related tasks. Many of these limitations come from how current large language models are designed and trained.

Section 8.1 focuses on limitations related to the design of large language models. Certain tasks, such as exact calculations and data processing, are difficult for AI tools because language models are not designed for these purposes.

Section 8.2 examines how the training process of language models affects the knowledge of AI tools. Language models can only partially store information from their training data and do not have access to the most recent information.

Section 8.3 discusses the issue of identifying sources for AI-generated answers. While large language models can create new content, they can also memorize text passages from their training data and repeat them directly.

8.1 Model Limitations

8.1.1 Hallucination

Consider the following discussion about a data structure called an *AVL list* which combines some features of AVL trees and linked lists:

> *Prompt*: I would like to use the well-known AVL list data structure in my algorithm (it combines the strengths of AVL trees and linked lists). What is the time complexity for adding a new element to an AVL list?
>
> *Answer*: An AVL list is a data structure that combines the properties of AVL trees and linked lists, aiming to provide efficient access and modification operations. The AVL list maintains the balanced tree property of AVL trees while allowing for efficient sequential access like a linked list.

> The time complexity for adding a new element to an AVL list generally depends on the position where the element is inserted:
>
> - Insertion at a specific index: If you are inserting at a specific index, the AVL list needs to find the correct position to maintain its balanced tree structure. This involves traversing the tree to find the insertion point, which takes $O(\log n)$ time due to the balanced nature of the AVL tree. After finding the correct position, the insertion operation itself, including any necessary rotations to maintain balance, also takes $O(\log n)$ time.
> - Insertion at the beginning or end: If you are inserting at the beginning or end of the list, the operation can be optimized. Inserting at the end typically involves finding the last node, which can be done in $O(\log n)$ time, followed by the insertion process that also takes $O(\log n)$ time. Inserting at the beginning might involve similar operations depending on how the AVL list is implemented.
>
> Overall, the time complexity for adding a new element to an AVL list is $O(\log n)$, where n is the number of elements in the list. This complexity arises from the need to maintain the balanced tree structure of the AVL list during insertion.

The problem here is that there is no data structure called AVL list: we just made it up. The generated answer combines some elements of AVL trees and linked lists, which are real data structures, but as a whole, the answer does not make sense. This is another example of hallucination in large language models.

One reason AI tools hallucinate is that their models are trained to predict the most probable next token in the sequence. In the example above, even though the model probably has no information about AVL lists, it might guess that such a data structure exists and use some facts about AVL trees and linked lists to describe how the structure could work.

Actually, the hallucination above is understandable. Suppose we are in a computer science exam, and there is a question about AVL lists—a topic we have not heard of. If we know about AVL trees and linked lists, we can invent something and try to get at least partial points for the question. If we simply say that we do not know about AVL lists, we will certainly not get any points. Similarly, a good strategy for AI can be to guess what the AVL list could be, instead of simply admitting that it does not know about it.

To continue the above example, if we write our prompt in a different way, we can get a very different answer:

> *Prompt*: My friend said there is a data structure called AVL list, but I don't know if it's a joke or not. Do you know such a data structure?
>
> *Answer*: It sounds like your friend might be joking or confused. There is no widely recognized data structure called an "AVL list." However, there is a well-known data structure called an "AVL tree." An AVL tree is a type of self-balancing binary search tree, named after its inventors Adelson-Velsky and Landis. In an AVL tree, the heights of the two child subtrees of any node differ by at most one, ensuring that the tree remains balanced. This balance allows for operations like insertion, deletion, and lookup to be performed in $O(\log n)$ time.
>
> If your friend mentioned an "AVL list," they may have been referring to an AVL tree or mixing it up with another data structure, such as a linked list.

8.1.2 Mathematical Tasks

A popular way to "prove" that AI tools are stupid is to create a social media post showing a screenshot where AI gives a wrong answer to a simple mathematical task. Indeed, calculations seem to be difficult for large language models. For example, consider the following discussion:

Prompt: What is 19^{19}?

Answer: 19^{19} is a very large number. Calculating it gives:
$$19^{19} = 1,978,419,655,660,313,449.$$

Prompt: This is not correct. Can you try again?

Answer: Apologies for the mistake. Let's calculate 19^{19} again:
$$19^{19} = 1,978,419,655,660,313,456.$$
Thank you for pointing that out.

Prompt: This is not correct. Can you try again?

Answer: Apologies for the mistake. Apologies for the previous errors. Let's calculate 19^{19} correctly this time:
$$19^{19} = 1,978,419,655,660,313,529.$$
Thank you for your patience.

It seems that we get a different answer every time. Each answer has the same prefix, but none of the answers is correct. The second suggested answer is especially poor because it is not possible for the product of the odd number 19 multiplied by itself to end with the digit 6. Here is the correct answer, which has the same prefix but is much larger than the AI-generated answers:

$$19^{19} = 1,978,419,655,660,313,589,123,979.$$

Here is another example where we try to find the prime factors of a number:

Prompt: What are the prime factors of 1545013?

Answer: The prime factors of 1545013 are 13, 17, and 69733.

The generated answer is not correct because $13 \cdot 17 \cdot 69733 = 15410993$, which is different from 1545013. In fact, 69733 is not even a valid prime factor because $137 \cdot 509 = 69733$. The actual prime factors of 1545013 are 1237 and 1249.

Why can language models give high-quality answers to complex questions, but they cannot solve simple mathematical problems? The reason is that language models have been trained to generate language, not act as calculators. Language models can solve tasks that humans can solve. Most people could not calculate the value of 19^{19} or find the prime factors of 1545013, so it makes sense that language models also have trouble with such tasks.

On the other hand, we can use language models to create code that solves mathematical problems correctly. For example, we can generate the following solutions to the problems above:

Prompt: Create Python code that calculates the value of 19^{19}.

Answer: Calculating the value of 19^{19} in Python is straightforward using the exponentiation operator **. Here's a simple script to perform this calculation:

```python
# Calculate 19 to the power of 19
result = 19 ** 19

# Print the result
print("The value of 19^19 is:", result)
```

When you run this code, it will compute 19^{19} and print the result. Python handles large integers well, so you don't need to worry about integer overflow with this calculation.

Prompt: Create Python code that finds the prime factors of 1545013.

Answer: To find the prime factors of a number in Python, you can use a simple algorithm that checks divisibility from the smallest prime number (2) upwards. Here's a Python function that accomplishes this task:

```python
def prime_factors(n):
    factors = []
    # Start with the smallest prime number
    divisor = 2
    
    while n >= 2:
        if n % divisor == 0:
            factors.append(divisor)
            n //= divisor
        else:
            divisor += 1
    
    return factors

# Test the function with the number 1545013
number = 1545013
factors = prime_factors(number)
print("Prime factors of", number, "are:", factors)
```

8.1 Model Limitations

> This function will iterate through possible divisors starting from 2 and check if the number is divisible by the current divisor. If it is, it adds the divisor to the list of factors and divides the number by the divisor. If not, it increments the divisor and continues the process. The loop stops when the number is reduced to 1.
> Running this code will give you the prime factors of 1545013.

This is the way a human programmer could also solve the above problems. Some AI tools already use this technique by calling, for example, a Python interpreter when they need to do exact calculations.

8.1.3 Data Processing

Another difficult task for language models is processing data accurately, especially when the amount of data is large. Suppose we have a text file that contains words and we want to count the number of unique words. Let's try to give the data to AI and ask it to count the words:

Prompt: Count the number of distinct words in the following data:

```
monkey
banana
banana
harpsichord
monkey
banana
monkey
harpsichord
banana
```

Answer: To count the number of distinct words in the provided data, we can first list the words and then identify the unique ones. The words in the data are:

monkey, banana, banana, harpsichord, monkey, banana, monkey, harpsichord, banana
Now, let's identify the distinct words:
monkey, banana, harpsichord
Thus, the distinct words are monkey, banana, and harpsichord.
In total, there are 3 distinct words.

The generated answer is correct, so let's try to do the same with a larger amount of data. In the following prompt, the list of words consists of 1,000 random strings made up of the letters "a" and "b":

> *Prompt*: Count the number of distinct words in the following data:
>
> ```
> ababbaabbb
> aaabbaaaba
> baabbaaaaa
> abbbbbabbb
> ababbbbbaa
> [...]
> ```
>
> *Answer*: To count the number of distinct words in the provided data, we can use a set to collect unique words as we iterate through the list. Below is a summary of the process:
>
> - Read each word from the data.
> - Add each word to a set (which automatically handles duplicates).
> - Finally, count the number of unique words in the set.
>
> Let's proceed with the counting.
> After analyzing the provided data, the number of distinct words is 343.

Is 343 the correct answer? Actually, if we use the same prompt five times, we get five different answers: 343, 222, 625, 420, and 565, which shows we cannot trust AI in this task. Since the amount of data is large, it would be very difficult to know which answer (if any) is correct.[1]

The problem with this approach is that processing data is another task that language models are not well suited for because of their design and limited context size. Tasks where exact counting is needed are often difficult for language models. Again, we should remember that language models and humans have similar skills and weaknesses. Counting the number of unique words in a list of 1,000 random strings without extra help would also be a very difficult task for humans.

Also in this task, we can phrase the prompt differently to get instructions for calculating the exact number of distinct words:

> *Prompt*: I have a text file that contains words, one word each line. How can I count the number of distinct words using Unix tools?
>
> *Answer*: You can count the number of distinct words in a text file using a combination of Unix command-line tools. Here's a simple way to do it using `sort` and `uniq`:

---

[1] Actually, since we know how the data has been generated, we can calculate the expected number of distinct words using the formula $\sum_{i=1}^{n} \left(\frac{t-1}{t}\right)^{i-1}$, where n is the number of words in the list and t is the number of possible words. The idea of the formula is to calculate, for each word, the probability that it is different from all previous words. In our case, $n = 1000$ and $t = 2^{10}$, which gives about 638.54. This suggests that some of the answers are clearly too small, but 625 *could* be a correct answer.

```
sort yourfile.txt | uniq | wc -l
```

Here's what each part of the command does:

- `sort yourfile.txt`: This sorts the lines in the file `yourfile.txt`. Sorting is necessary because uniq only removes consecutive duplicate lines.
- `uniq`: This command filters out the repeated lines that are adjacent to each other, leaving only unique lines.
- `wc -l`: This counts the number of lines in the output from the previous command, which corresponds to the number of distinct words.

Using the proposed method, we can find out that the actual number of distinct words in the file is 643.

8.2 Knowledge Limitations

8.2.1 Missing Knowledge

A language model can only know things that it has learned from its training data. In the following example, we ask a specific question about a feature in Survo, a computing environment developed in Finland.

> *Prompt*: How is the `INTREL` feature used in Survo?
>
> *Answer*: Survo is a versatile software environment primarily used for statistical analysis, data management, and related computational tasks. One of its features is `INTREL`, which stands for interactive relational database management. `INTREL` is used to manage and manipulate relational data within Survo.
> Here's how `INTREL` can be utilized in Survo: [...]

This answer is hallucinated: the `INTREL` feature is not related to database management, but is used to find integer relations.[2] While some information about Survo has clearly been included in the training data, it is possible that this feature does not appear at all in the training data.

Also, if something has changed after the language model was trained, the model cannot know about it. For example, the knowledge cutoff for OpenAI's GPT-4o model is October 2023, which means it does not know about Python versions released after that. The following prompt also shows this:

---

[2] https://www.survo.fi/help/qmi1_01.html.

> *Prompt*: What is the latest Python version you know?
>
> *Answer*: The latest Python version I am aware of is Python 3.11, which was officially released on October 24, 2022. However, Python 3.12 is expected to be released in October 2023. For the most up-to-date information, you should check the official Python website or their release calendar.

Let's test what happens when we ask about a Python language feature released after Python 3.11. One such feature is the `sumprod` function, which was added to the `math` module in Python 3.12. The function can be used to calculate the sum of products of elements from two lists. For example, given the lists [1, 2, 3] and [4, 5, 6], the result is $1 \cdot 4 + 2 \cdot 5 + 3 \cdot 6 = 32$.

> *Prompt*: How could I use the `sumprod` function in the Python `math` module?
>
> *Answer*: The `math` module in Python does not have a `sumprod` function. However, you can achieve the functionality of summing the product of elements from two lists using other approaches in Python.
>
> If you want to calculate the sum of the products of corresponding elements in two lists, you can use a combination of `zip` and a generator expression or list comprehension. Here's an example of how you can do this:
>
> ```
> # Define two lists
> list1 = [1, 2, 3, 4]
> list2 = [5, 6, 7, 8]
>
> # Calculate the sum of products using a generator expression
> sum_product = sum(x * y for x, y in zip(list1, list2))
>
> print(sum_product)   # Output: 70
> ```
>
> In this example, `zip(list1, list2)` pairs up corresponding elements from `list1` and `list2`, and the generator expression `x * y for x, y in zip(list1, list2)` calculates the product of each pair. The `sum` function then adds up these products to give the final result.

Indeed, the GPT-4o model does not know that the `math` module now includes the `sumprod` function. However, it manages to guess what the function should do and shows how the same result could be achieved using other Python features.

While language models only know what is in their training data, AI tools can provide them with more information, just as the user can add more details in the prompt. For example, some AI tools can perform web searches, and the results can be used as extra material when creating answers.

8.2.2 Knowledge Depth

In general, the more popular a programming language is, the better language models know it because there is more training data available for popular languages. For example, AI tools are good at generating code in popular languages, such as JavaScript and Python, but they may struggle with less commonly used languages, such as Forth and Nim.

Even if some topic has been part of the training data, it is not guaranteed that all relevant information about the topic is stored and available in the language model. It can also be difficult to create prompts that get all the information that the model might have about a specific topic.

As an example, suppose we need to verify email addresses and want to know the definition of a valid email address. We can try to use the following prompt to get the definition:

Prompt: What is the definition of a valid email address?

Answer: A valid email address typically follows a specific format defined by the Internet standards, primarily the RFC 5322 specification. Here are the key components of a valid email address:

1. Local Part: This is the portion before the "@" symbol. It can include:

   - Letters (uppercase and lowercase)
   - Numbers
   - Special characters such as # $ % & ' * + - / = ? ^ { | } ~
   - Dots (.) are allowed, but they cannot be the first or last character, nor can they appear consecutively.

2. "@" Symbol: This separates the local part from the domain part.
3. Domain Part: This follows the "@" symbol and consists of:

   - Domain names, which can include letters, numbers, and hyphens (-).
   - Dots (.) to separate domain levels (e.g., subdomain, domain, top-level domain).
   - A valid domain typically ends with a top-level domain (TLD) like .com, .org, .net, etc.

   Additional considerations include:

- The total length of the email address should not exceed 254 characters.
- The local part should not exceed 64 characters.
- The domain part should not exceed 255 characters.
- The email address should not contain spaces or special characters outside of the allowed set.

These rules ensure that email addresses can be correctly interpreted and routed by email systems.

This answer contains useful information but it is vague. For example, we do not know if the list of special characters is complete or if the list of additional considerations is complete. The answer also contains some hallucination: it claims that the maximum total length of the address is 254 characters, but the maximum length of the domain part (which is part of the address) is 255 characters.

We can try to get more details by using additional prompts, such as:

Prompt: Are there any allowed special characters other than those listed in your answer?

Answer: Yes, there are additional special characters that are allowed in the local part of an email address according to the RFC standards. Besides those I mentioned earlier, you can also use:

- . (dot) – but not at the beginning or end, and not consecutively.
- " (quotation marks)–can be used to enclose the entire local part if special characters are included.
- (,), , , :, ;, <, >, @, [,], \ – these characters can be used within quoted strings or with escape sequences.

It's important to note that while these characters are technically allowed, many email systems and providers impose additional restrictions for practical reasons, such as compatibility and security. Therefore, using more common characters like letters, numbers, and simple symbols (e.g., . or _) is advisable for ensuring compatibility across different systems.

However, the problem is that even if we use several prompts to ask for more information, we can never be sure that we have obtained all the necessary information. For a task like the one above, we should read the original source instead of trying to collect information piece by piece from AI. In the example above, the generated answer even includes the source we should read: the RFC 5322 document, which contains the definition of an email address.

8.3 Generalization Versus Memorization

It is not well understood how large language models actually store the information they have learned. Ideally, the models would learn to *generalize* the information in the training data so that they can create new content using it. However, it has been observed that the models also *memorize* training material and they may repeat long sections from it word for word.

8.3 Generalization Versus Memorization

Unusual methods have been developed to detect memorization. In a study [1], researchers found that when the version of ChatGPT at that time was asked to repeat a certain word (such as the word "book" in their experiment), it might first repeat the word as requested, but then deviate from the instructions and start producing random text, which could include passages copied directly from websites.

One problem with memorization is that using AI-generated content may lead to a situation where someone else's work is used without permission or credit. For example, suppose you generate some code using AI, and it is later found that the code was directly copied from someone else's project. It is not clear how likely it is that this could happen.

In general, it is difficult to find sources for AI-generated content. As an example, consider the task of implementing an AVL tree[3] data structure in Python. Here is part of an implementation generated by AI:

Prompt: How can I implement an AVL tree in Python?

Answer: An AVL tree is a self-balancing binary search tree where the difference between heights of left and right subtrees cannot be more than one for all nodes. Here's a basic implementation in Python:

```
[...]
        # Left Left Case
        if balance > 1 and key < root.left.key:
            return self.right_rotate(root)

        # Right Right Case
        if balance < -1 and key > root.right.key:
            return self.left_rotate(root)

        # Left Right Case
        if balance > 1 and key > root.left.key:
            root.left = self.left_rotate(root.left)
            return self.right_rotate(root)

        # Right Left Case
        if balance < -1 and key < root.right.key:
            root.right = self.right_rotate(root.right)
            return self.left_rotate(root)

        # Return the unchanged root pointer
        return root
[...]
```

Next, let's try to find the source of the implementation:

---

[3] Unlike the previously discussed AVL list, the AVL tree is a real data structure that can be used to implement an efficiently working binary search tree.

> *Prompt*: What is the source of your implementation?
>
> *Answer*: The AVL tree implementation provided is a standard approach commonly found in computer science textbooks, tutorials, and online resources. It is based on the well-known algorithm for maintaining balance in a binary search tree using rotations. The code structure and logic are derived from the principles of AVL trees, which were introduced by Georgy Adelson-Velsky and Evgenii Landis in 1962.
>   The implementation is a synthesis of typical practices used in programming AVL trees in Python, and it is not directly sourced from a specific publication or website. It reflects the general methodology for AVL tree operations like insertion, rotation, and height calculation. If you need a specific source or reference, many computer science resources cover AVL trees, such as "Introduction to Algorithms" by Cormen et al., or online educational platforms like GeeksforGeeks, TutorialsPoint, and others that provide similar explanations and code examples.

No single source for the code is reported, but some possible sources are given, such as the GeeksForGeeks platform. In fact, GeeksForGeeks has an article called *Insertion in an AVL Tree*,[4] which includes an AVL tree implementation in Python. Surprisingly, the GeeksForGeeks implementation is almost identical to the AI-generated implementation:

```python
[...]
    # Left Left Case
    if balance > 1 and key < node.left.key:
        return right_rotate(node)

    # Right Right Case
    if balance < -1 and key > node.right.key:
        return left_rotate(node)

    # Left Right Case
    if balance > 1 and key > node.left.key:
        node.left = left_rotate(node.left)
        return right_rotate(node)

    # Right Left Case
    if balance < -1 and key < node.right.key:
        node.right = right_rotate(node.right)
        return left_rotate(node)

    # Return the (unchanged) node pointer
    return node
[...]
```

What is happening here? At first, it looks like the GeeksForGeeks article was used as training data, and the language model has almost directly memorized the code, which it now reproduced. However, there is another possibility: the author of the

---

[4] https://www.geeksforgeeks.org/dsa/insertion-in-an-avl-tree/.

GeeksForGeeks article may have generated the example code for the article using AI. In fact, more and more code on the internet is AI-generated, which makes the line between "original" and "AI-generated" code unclear.

Reference

1. M. Nasr, N. Carlini, et al., Scalable extraction of training data from (production) language models (2023). arXiv:2311.17035

Software Development 9

This chapter focuses on using generative AI to efficiently create components we need in software development. In general, AI tools are great at generating code for small, well-specified components, such as functions and classes.

Section 9.1 explores a fundamental challenge when using AI tools in software development: describing our context so that AI understands our goals. For example, generating proof-of-concept code or production code are two very different tasks.

Section 9.2 provides examples of creating well-specified components. For example, we can create functions by describing their parameters and return values, and classes by listing the methods they should contain.

Section 9.3 discusses an experiment where we create a word game web application using generative AI. First, we build the skeleton of the game, and then we add new features by asking AI to generate the components we need.

9.1 Describing Context

Describing our context clearly enough when using AI tools is difficult. We often have some expectations that we do not mention in the prompt, such as the intended use of the code that should be generated. Even worse, AI tools often do not ask clarifying questions, and instead guess the missing details.

This can lead to a situation where it seems to us that AI cannot generate a good answer related to our topic. However, it is possible that the answer could be good in some other context, and the real problem is that the context has not been specified.

As an example, consider the following prompt where our goal is to create a PHP page for a web application. The code should store messages sent through a web form in a database.

Prompt: Create a PHP page where the user can send a message through a web form, and the message is stored in a database.

Answer: Here's a compact PHP example for a web form that allows users to send a message, which is then stored in a MySQL database.
First, create a table in your MySQL database to store messages:

```sql
CREATE TABLE messages (
    id INT AUTO_INCREMENT PRIMARY KEY,
    message TEXT NOT NULL,
    created_at TIMESTAMP DEFAULT CURRENT_TIMESTAMP
);
```

Then, create a file named `message_form.php`:

```php
<?php
$host = 'localhost'; // Database host
$db = 'your_database'; // Database name
$user = 'your_username'; // Database username
$pass = 'your_password'; // Database password

// Create connection
$conn = new mysqli($host, $user, $pass, $db);

// Check connection
if ($conn->connect_error) {
    die("Connection failed: " . $conn->connect_error);
}

// Handle form submission
if ($_SERVER["REQUEST_METHOD"] == "POST") {
    $message = $conn->real_escape_string($_POST['message']);
    $sql = "INSERT INTO messages (message) VALUES ('$message')";
    if ($conn->query($sql) === TRUE) {
        echo "Message sent successfully!";
    } else {
        echo "Error: " . $sql . "<br>" . $conn->error;
    }
}

$conn->close();
?>
[...]
```

From the viewpoint of a professional web developer, there are several problems in the generated code:

- It is not a good practice to include the database connection code in the same page that shows and handles the message form.
- Using the method `real_escape_string` is an old-fashioned and questionable way to prevent SQL injection.
- The form input is not validated. For example, someone could send a message with a million characters, and it would be stored in the database.

9.1 Describing Context

In short, the generated code is more like a proof of concept than production-level code. However, we have not told the AI how we will use the code. If our goal is to create production-level code, this is part of the context that only exists in our mind. We could have a different context that would match the code above: for example, we might just need some standalone PHP code for testing.

Here is a new version of the prompt that defines our context better. This time, we mention that we want to generate production-level code, and we also provide more information about our environment and requirements.

Prompt: Create a PHP page where the user can send a message through a web form, and the message is stored in a database.

Create professional code which could be used in production. Assume that there is a file database.php that handles the database connection. There is a function query($sql, $params) available. Remember to validate inputs.

Answer: Here's a PHP page that allows users to send a message through a web form. The message is stored in a database using the provided query($sql, $params) function. The code includes input validation for security.

```php
<?php
require 'database.php';

if ($_SERVER['REQUEST_METHOD'] === 'POST') {
    $message = trim($_POST['message'] ?? '');

    // Validate input
    if (empty($message)) {
        $error = "Message cannot be empty.";
    } elseif (strlen($message) > 500) {
        $error = "Message cannot exceed 500 characters.";
    } else {
        // Store message in the database
        $sql = "INSERT INTO messages (content) VALUES (:content)";
        query($sql, ['content' => $message]);
        $success = "Message sent successfully!";
    }
}
?>
[...]
```

Alternatively, even if AI tools do not usually ask further questions before implementing code, we can create a prompt that encourages them to ask more details about our requirements before generating code.

> *Prompt*: Create a PHP page where the user can send a message through a web form, and the message is stored in a database.
> However, before creating any code, please ask me for more details about my requirements.
>
> *Answer*: Sure, I'd be happy to help you create a PHP page for sending and storing messages. Here are some questions to better understand your requirements:
>
> 1. What is the purpose of the messaging feature?
> 2. Do you have a preferred database system (e.g., MySQL, PostgreSQL)?
> 3. Should the message include any additional fields (e.g., subject, timestamp)?
> 4. Do you have any specific security requirements (e.g., input validation, sanitization)?
> 5. Is user authentication required for sending messages?
> 6. Do you need a way to view or manage messages after they are stored?
> 7. Are there any design or styling preferences for the web form?
> 8. Should the form include any validation or error handling mechanisms?
> 9. Will the application be hosted on a specific server or environment?
> 10. Do you have any existing code or frameworks you'd like to integrate?

9.2 Creating Components

A difficulty in software development is complexity, and a well-known method to deal with complexity is to divide the application into components that are small enough and have clearly defined responsibilities [1].

This way of thinking is also useful when using AI tools. When we have identified a small component that is needed in our application and can define what the component should do, we can create a specification that AI can use to generate such a component.

For example, the following prompt describes the parameters of a function and what the function should return.

> *Prompt*: Create a Python function `find_common_words` that is given two word lists as parameters. The function returns a sorted list that consists of all words that appear in both input lists.
>
> *Answer*: You can create a Python function `find_common_words` that takes two lists of words as parameters and returns a sorted list of common words. Here is a sample implementation:
>
> ```
> def find_common_words(list1, list2):
>     set1 = set(list1)
>     set2 = set(list2)
>
>     common_words = set1.intersection(set2)
>
>     return sorted(common_words)
> ```

9.2 Creating Components

Similarly, we can create a class that consists of methods by providing the list of methods the class should have. For example, the following prompt generates a class for finding routes between cities.

Prompt: Create a Python class `RouteFinder` that contains the following methods:

- `add_city(name)`: adds a city with a given name
- `add_road(city1, city2)`: adds a road between two cities
- `find_route(city1, city2)`: finds a route from city1 to city2 and returns a list that contains all cities on the route

Answer: Here's a Python class `RouteFinder` that implements the requested functionality. The class allows you to add cities, create roads between them, and find routes from one city to another using a breadth-first search algorithm.

```python
from collections import deque

class RouteFinder:
    def __init__(self):
        self.cities = set()
        self.roads = {}

    def add_city(self, name):
        self.cities.add(name)
        self.roads[name] = []

    def add_road(self, city1, city2):
        self.roads[city1].append(city2)
        self.roads[city2].append(city1)

    def find_route(self, city1, city2):
        queue = deque([(city1, [city1])])   # (current city, path)
        visited = set()

        while queue:
            current_city, path = queue.popleft()
            visited.add(current_city)

            if current_city == city2:
                return path

            for neighbor in self.roads[current_city]:
                if neighbor not in visited:
                    queue.append((neighbor, path + [neighbor]))

        return None
```

Here is a more complex example of a function that uses the above `RouteFinder` class to find a route between two cities and shows the route on a map using the Pygame library. We specify each parameter of the function and describe how the function should draw the route.

Prompt: Create a Python function that is given the following parameters:

- a string that specifies a PNG file that contains a map of cities and roads
- a list of cities that consists of tuples, each element is of the form (name, x, y) where name is the name of the city and x and y are the coordinates of the city in the map
- a RouteFinder object that has a method find_route(city1, city2) that returns a route from city1 to city2 as a list that contains all city names on the route
- two strings: the first and last city on the route

The function should use Pygame to show the route on the map. The route should consists of lines between cities, drawn with red thick lines.

Answer: To create a Python function that displays a route on a map using Pygame, we first need to ensure that we have the Pygame library installed and that we have a suitable PNG map file. The function will utilize the RouteFinder object to retrieve the route between two specified cities and then draw that route on the map.

```python
import pygame

def display_route_on_map(map_file, cities, route_finder,
                        start_city, end_city):
    pygame.init()

    map_image = pygame.image.load(map_file)
    map_width, map_height = map_image.get_size()

    screen = pygame.display.set_mode((map_width, map_height))

    city_positions = {name: (x, y) for name, x, y in cities}

    route = route_finder.find_route(start_city, end_city)

    running = True
    while running:
        for event in pygame.event.get():
            if event.type == pygame.QUIT:
                running = False

        screen.blit(map_image, (0, 0))

        for i in range(len(route) - 1):
            city1 = route[i]
            city2 = route[i + 1]
            pygame.draw.line(screen, (255, 0, 0),
                city_positions[city1], city_positions[city2], 5)

        pygame.display.flip()

    pygame.quit()
```

9.3 Experiment: Creating a Word Game

In the following experiment, our goal is to use AI to create a Tetris-like word game as a web application using HTML and JavaScript. Each block contains two adjacent letters, and the objective is to form horizontal and vertical words with the blocks. Like in Tetris, the player can move and rotate the blocks using the arrow keys.

9.3 Experiment: Creating a Word Game

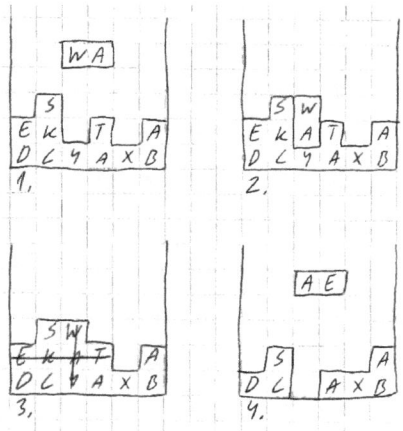

Fig. 9.1 A sketch for the game. The block with the letters W and A is rotated and placed, after which the words WAY and TAKE are formed and removed. The next block contains the letters A and E

After placing a block, both letters move as far down as possible on the board. Then, all horizontal and vertical words are identified, and all letters that are part of one or more words are removed. Finally, all remaining letters move down as far as possible, and the next block appears.

Figure 9.1 shows a more detailed sketch of how the game should work. The current block contains the letters W and A. After rotating and placing the block, the words WAY (vertical) and TAKE (horizontal, backwards) are formed. The letters that are part of the words are removed, and a new block with the letters A and E appears. Note that the letter S also moves one step down after the letters are removed.

9.3.1 Creating the Skeleton

We start by creating a skeleton for the game, which includes HTML code to show the game board and JavaScript code to create, move, and rotate the blocks during the game. In fact, creating the skeleton can be the most demanding part of the experiment because there are several elements that need to work together. Here is our first attempt to create the skeleton:

> *Prompt*: Create an HTML/JavaScript game that is like Tetris but each block consists of two adjacent squares with random letters.
> You can move the current block left and right using the arrow keys. You can also rotate the block using the up key.
>
> *Answer*: [...]

However, it turns out that the results using the prompt above are not satisfactory. The biggest problem seems to be that correctly implementing the rotation of the blocks is trickier than expected. After generating several versions of the code, a

Fig. 9.2 Four possible rotations of a block. The first letter A never moves, and the second letter B has four possible positions

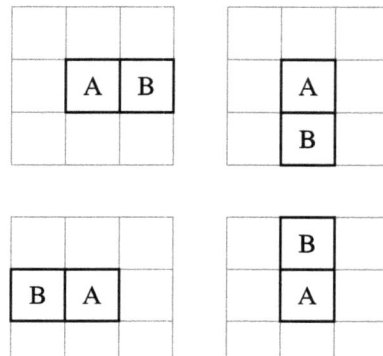

recurring problem is that when the player keeps rotating the block, the block slowly moves to the left or to the right, which should not happen.

The issue here is that we have not clearly specified what the rotation of the blocks means in this game. For a human programmer who has played Tetris and similar games, it is quite clear intuitively how the rotation should work, but how should we describe it?

After some time, we come up with the following definition: the first letter of a block does not move when rotating the block, and the second letter has four possible positions in four directions (Fig. 9.2). By using this definition in the prompt, we can finally create a good working skeleton for the game (Fig. 9.3).

Prompt: Create an HTML/JavaScript game that is like Tetris but each block consists of two adjacent squares with random letters.

You can move the current block left and right using the arrow keys. You can also rotate the block using the up key.

For each block, store the position of its first square and the direction that defines the position of the second square. The directions are: 0 = right, 1 = down, 2 = left, 3 = up. The position of the first square does not change when you rotate the block.

Answer: Here's a simple implementation of a Tetris-like game where each block consists of two adjacent squares, each with a random letter. The game allows you to move the blocks left and right using arrow keys and rotate them using the up arrow key.

You can copy and paste this code into an HTML file and open it in a web browser to play the game.
[...]

After some minor refactorings and changes to the generated code, the skeleton for our game is ready:

```
<!DOCTYPE html>
<html>
<head>
    <title>Word Game</title>
    <style>
```

9.3 Experiment: Creating a Word Game

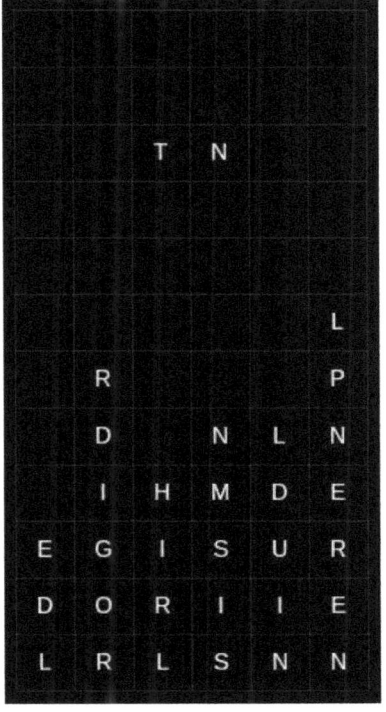

Fig. 9.3 The skeleton for the word game working in a web browser. The current block consists of letters T and N, and it can be moved and rotated using the arrow keys

```
        [...]
    </style>
</head>
<body>

<div id="game"></div>

<script>
    const width = 8;
    const height = 16;
    const gameElement = document.getElementById('game');
    const grid = Array.from({ length: height },
        () => Array(width).fill(null));
    let currentBlock = createBlock();
    let currentPosition = { x: 3, y: 0 };

    function generateLetter() {
        const letters = 'ABCDEFGHIJKLMNOPQRSTUVWXYZ';
        return letters[Math.floor(Math.random() * letters.length)];
    }

    function createBlock() {
        const letter1 = generateLetter();
        const letter2 = generateLetter();
        return {
            letters: [letter1, letter2],
            direction: 0 // 0 = right, 1 = down, 2 = left, 3 = up
        };
    }
```

```
function drawGrid() {
    gameElement.innerHTML = '';
    for (let y = 0; y < height; y++) {
        for (let x = 0; x < width; x++) {
            const cell = document.createElement('div');
            cell.className = 'cell';
            if (grid[y][x]) {
                cell.innerText = grid[y][x];
            }
            gameElement.appendChild(cell);
        }
    }
}

function secondSquarePosition(x, y, direction) {
    let secondX = x, secondY = y;
    if (direction === 0) secondX += 1;
    else if (direction === 1) secondY += 1;
    else if (direction === 2) secondX -= 1;
    else if (direction === 3) secondY -= 1;
    return [secondX, secondY];
}

function squareInBounds(x, y) {
    return y >= 0 && y < height && x >= 0 && x < width;
}

function drawBlock() {
    const { x, y } = currentPosition;
    const { letters, direction } = currentBlock;

    grid[y][x] = letters[0];

    const [secondX, secondY] = secondSquarePosition(x, y, direction);

    if (squareInBounds(secondX, secondY)) {
        grid[secondY][secondX] = letters[1];
    }

    drawGrid();
}

function clearBlock() {
    const { x, y } = currentPosition;
    const { direction } = currentBlock;

    grid[y][x] = null;

    const [secondX, secondY] = secondSquarePosition(x, y, direction);

    if (squareInBounds(secondX, secondY)) {
        grid[secondY][secondX] = null;
    }

    drawGrid();
}

function moveBlock(dx, dy) {
    clearBlock();
    const originalPosition = { ...currentPosition };
    currentPosition.x += dx;
    currentPosition.y += dy;
    if (isColliding()) {
        currentPosition = originalPosition;
    }
    drawBlock();
```

9.3 Experiment: Creating a Word Game

```
    }
    function rotateBlock() {
        clearBlock();
        const originalBlock = { ...currentBlock };
        currentBlock.direction = (currentBlock.direction + 1) % 4;
        if (isColliding()) {
            currentBlock = originalBlock;
        }
        drawBlock();
    }
    function isColliding() {
        const { x, y } = currentPosition;
        const { direction } = currentBlock;

        if (!squareInBounds(x, y)) return true;

        const [secondX, secondY] = secondSquarePosition(x, y, direction);

        return (!squareInBounds(secondX, secondY) ||
            grid[secondY][secondX]);
    }
    function dropBlock() {
        clearBlock();
        const originalPosition = { ...currentPosition };
        currentPosition.y += 1;
        if (isColliding()) {
            currentPosition = originalPosition;
            placeBlock();
            currentBlock = createBlock();
            currentPosition = { x: 3, y: 0 };
            if (isColliding()) {
                alert("Game Over!");
                resetGame();
            }
        }
        drawBlock();
    }
    function placeBlock() {
        const { x, y } = currentPosition;
        const { letters, direction } = currentBlock;
        grid[y][x] = letters[0];

        const [secondX, secondY] = secondSquarePosition(x, y, direction);

        if (squareInBounds(secondX, secondY)) {
            grid[secondY][secondX] = letters[1];
        }
    }
    function resetGame() {
        for (let y = 0; y < height; y++) {
            for (let x = 0; x < width; x++) {
                grid[y][x] = null;
            }
        }
        currentBlock = createBlock();
        currentPosition = { x: 3, y: 0 };
        drawGrid();
    }
    document.addEventListener('keydown', (event) => {
        if (event.key === 'ArrowLeft') {
            moveBlock(-1, 0);
```

```
            } else if (event.key === 'ArrowRight') {
                moveBlock(1, 0);
            } else if (event.key === 'ArrowUp') {
                rotateBlock();
            }
        });

        setInterval(() => {
            dropBlock();
        }, 1000);

        drawBlock();
    </script>
</body>
</html>
```

9.3.2 Adding More Features

Now the skeleton for the game is ready, and we can start adding more features to the game. We will describe each new feature as a function or class that has a clear task.

The first feature to add is related to what happens after placing a block in the game. If the block is in a horizontal position, both letters should be moved down as far as possible in their columns. Similarly, after detecting a word and removing a letter, the letters above the removed letter should be moved as far down as possible. We can handle both tasks by creating a function that moves the letters as far down as possible in each column.

> *Prompt*: Create a function moveLetters that modifies a two-dimensional array grid where each element is null or a letter. For each column, all letters should be moved as down as possible.
>
> *Answer*: Below is a function called moveLetters that takes a two-dimensional array grid as input and modifies it so that all letters in each column are moved down as far as possible. The function will iterate through each column, collect the letters, and then fill the bottom of the column with those letters, leaving the upper part of the column as null.
>
> ```
> function moveLetters() {
>     const height = grid.length;
>     const width = grid[0].length;
>
>     for (let col = 0; col < width; col++) {
>         const letters = [];
>
>         // Collect all letters in the current column
>         for (let row = 0; row < height; row++) {
>             if (grid[row][col] !== null) {
>                 letters.push(grid[row][col]);
>             }
>         }
>
>         // Clear the column
>         for (let row = 0; row < height; row++) {
>             grid[row][col] = null;
> ```

9.3 Experiment: Creating a Word Game

```
        }
            // Place letters at the bottom of the column
            for (let i = 0; i < letters.length; i++) {
                grid[height - 1 - i][col] =
                    letters[letters.length - 1 - i];
            }
        }
    }
}
```

The generated function `moveLetters` works by adding the letters in each column to a list and then placing the letters back into the grid in reverse order.

Next, let's focus on detecting the words in the grid. We have a text file that contains a list of valid words. First, we need a way to read the words from the file, with each word on a separate line. We will create a function that reads the words from the file and returns them as a list. In this context, it is good to mention that we are creating a browser application, and the word list is stored in a remote file.

Prompt: Create a JavaScript function that reads a list of words from a file and returns them as a list. The function should work in a browser and read the words from a remote file.

Answer: To create a JavaScript function that reads a list of words from a remote file and returns them as a list, you can use the Fetch API to retrieve the contents of the file. Below is an example function that accomplishes this. The function assumes the words in the file are separated by new lines.

```
async function fetchWordsFromFile(url) {
    try {
        // Fetch the file from the provided URL
        const response = await fetch(url);

        // Check if the response is ok
        if (!response.ok) {
            throw new Error('HTTP error ${response.status}');
        }

        // Read the response text
        const text = await response.text();

        // Split the text into an array of words
        const words = text.split('\n')
                        .map(word => word.trim().toUpperCase())
                        .filter(word => word.length >= 3);

        return words;
    } catch (error) {
        console.error('Error fetching words:', error);
        return [];
    }
}
```

The resulting function `fetchWordsFromFile` uses the Fetch API for reading data from a file, which is a good solution to this task.

After placing a block, the game should detect any words that can be formed using the letters in the grid. A basic way to do this would be to check all possible ways to

Fig. 9.4 A trie that contains the strings CANAL, CANDY, THE, and THERE

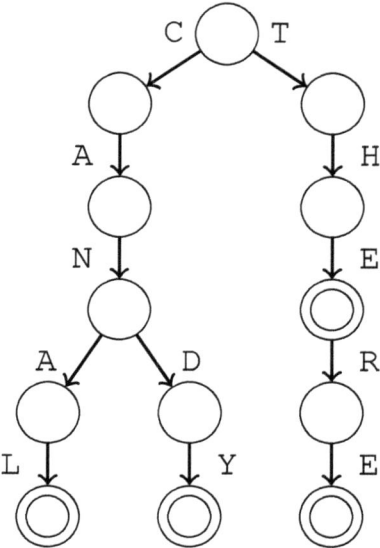

form words in the grid and use the list of words to detect the valid words. However, because there are many possible words, we probably need a more efficient method. In this case, it is a good idea to suggest a suitable data structure for the task when generating the code for detecting words.

An efficient and simple data structure for detecting words is a trie, shown in Fig. 9.4. A trie stores a set of words as a tree structure. We can build the trie efficiently and use it to search for words or their prefixes. Let's create a JavaScript class that implements the trie data structure:

Prompt: Show code for creating a trie data structure using JavaScript.

Answer: Here's a simple implementation of a Trie in JavaScript:

```
class TrieNode {
    constructor() {
        this.children = {};
        this.isEndOfWord = false;
    }
}

class Trie {
    constructor() {
        this.root = new TrieNode();
    }

    // Insert a word into the Trie
    insert(word) {
        let node = this.root;

        for (let char of word) {
```

9.3 Experiment: Creating a Word Game

```
            if (!node.children[char]) {
                node.children[char] = new TrieNode();
            }
            node = node.children[char];
        }
        node.isEndOfWord = true;
    }

    // Search for a word in the Trie
    search(word) {
        let node = this.root;
        for (let char of word) {
            if (!node.children[char]) {
                return false;
            }
            node = node.children[char];
        }
        return node.isEndOfWord;
    }
}
```

This is a good trie implementation which provides the method `insert` for adding a new word to the trie and the method `search` for searching for a word. We can convert the word list into a trie as follows:

Prompt: Create a function `createTrie` that is given a list of words and returns a trie (as defined above) that contains the words.

Answer: We can create a function `createTrie` that takes an array of words as input and constructs a Trie using the previously defined `Trie` and `TrieNode` classes. Here's how you can implement this function:

```
function createTrie(words) {
    const trie = new Trie();
    for (const word of words) {
        trie.insert(word);
    }
    return trie;
}
```

A more difficult part is using the trie to detect the words in the grid. In this case, it is good to describe exactly what we want to do: what is the input for the function and what the function should produce.

Prompt: Create a function that is given two things:

- a two-dimensional grid where each element is null or a letter
- a trie that contains words

The function should return a list of all occurrences of words in the grid. Each occurrence is horizontal or vertical and both directions are allowed. For each occurrence, include the coordinates of the first and last letter in the grid.

Answer: To solve this problem, we can create a function that searches for words in a two-dimensional grid using the provided Trie. The function will check for words horizontally (both left-to-right and right-to-left) and vertically (both top-to-bottom and bottom-to-top).

```
function findWordsInGrid(grid, trie) {
    const results = [];
    const rows = grid.length;
    const cols = grid[0].length;

    // Helper function to search in one direction
    const searchInDirection = (startRow, startCol, dRow, dCol) => {
        let word = '';
        let row = startRow;
        let col = startCol;

        while (row >= 0 && row < rows && col >= 0 && col < cols) {
            word += grid[row][col];
            if (trie.search(word)) {
                // If the word is found, store the coordinates
                results.push([[startRow, startCol], [row, col]]);
            }
            row += dRow;
            col += dCol;
        }
    };

    // Check all starting points in the grid
    for (let row = 0; row < rows; row++) {
        for (let col = 0; col < cols; col++) {
            if (grid[row][col] !== null) {
                // Horizontal: left to right
                searchInDirection(row, col, 0, 1);
                // Horizontal: right to left
                searchInDirection(row, col, 0, -1);
                // Vertical: top to bottom
                searchInDirection(row, col, 1, 0);
                // Vertical: bottom to top
                searchInDirection(row, col, -1, 0);
            }
        }
    }
    return results;
}
```

The resulting function findWordsInGrid checks every possible starting position of a word in the grid to find the words. Note that there would be ways to detect the words more efficiently. For example, we could focus only on words that include a

9.3 Experiment: Creating a Word Game

letter from the last added block, or use the trie more efficiently instead of searching for each partial word separately. However, for now, let's use the simple implementation.

We also need a function to remove the letters that belong to one or more word occurrences. We can create the function as follows:

Prompt: We have a two-dimensional grid where each element is a letter or `null`. We also have a list of pairs that specify starting and ending coordinates of word occurrences. Create a function `processOccurrences` that goes through the occurrences and removes all letters in the occurrences.

Answer: You can create a JavaScript function called `processOccurrences` that takes a two-dimensional grid and an array of occurrences (each defined by a pair of starting and ending coordinates) and removes all letters in those occurrences by replacing them with `null`. Here is a sample implementation:

```javascript
function processOccurrences(occurrences) {
    // Loop through each occurrence
    for (const [start, end] of occurrences) {
        const [startRow, startCol] = start;
        const [endRow, endCol] = end;

        // Determine the direction of the occurrence
        if (startRow === endRow) {
            // Horizontal occurrence
            const row = startRow;
            const colStart = Math.min(startCol, endCol);
            const colEnd = Math.max(startCol, endCol);
            for (let col = colStart; col <= colEnd; col++) {
                grid[row][col] = null; // Remove the letter
            }
        } else if (startCol === endCol) {
            // Vertical occurrence
            const col = startCol;
            const rowStart = Math.min(startRow, endRow);
            const rowEnd = Math.max(startRow, endRow);
            for (let row = rowStart; row <= rowEnd; row++) {
                grid[row][col] = null; // Remove the letter
            }
        }
    }
}
```

There is one more simple way we can improve the game. At the moment, the distribution of the letters in blocks is uniform, which means each letter has the same chance to be chosen. This may not work well in practice, because letters appear with different frequencies in words. The game could become too hard if we have to use too many rare letters in words. We can use the word list to create a better distribution for the letters:

Prompt: Create a class that has two methods: setDistribution is given a list of words, and generateLetter generates a random letter based on the distribution.

Answer: To create a class that handles a letter distribution based on a given list of words, we can follow these steps:

1. Create the class with a method to set the distribution based on the given words.
2. Implement a method to generate a random letter based on the distribution.

Here's a sample implementation in JavaScript:

```javascript
class LetterDistribution {
    constructor() {
        this.letterCounts = {};
        this.totalLetters = 0;
    }

    // Method to set the distribution based on a list of words
    setDistribution(words) {
        this.letterCounts = {};
        this.totalLetters = 0;

        // Count the occurrences of each letter
        for (const word of words) {
            for (const letter of word) {
                if (this.letterCounts[letter]) {
                    this.letterCounts[letter]++;
                } else {
                    this.letterCounts[letter] = 1;
                }
                this.totalLetters++;
            }
        }
    }

    // Method to generate a random letter based on the distribution
    generateLetter() {
        if (this.totalLetters === 0) {
            throw new Error("Distribution is not set.");
        }

        // Generate a random number between 0 and totalLetters
        const randomNum = Math.floor(Math.random() * this.totalLetters);
        let cumulativeCount = 0;

        // Find the letter corresponding to the random number
        for (const letter in this.letterCounts) {
            cumulativeCount += this.letterCounts[letter];
            if (randomNum < cumulativeCount) {
                return letter;
            }
        }
    }
}
```

Here, the method setDistribution counts how many times each letter appears in the word list. Using this distribution, the method generateLetter creates a letter. This method can be used whenever a block with two letters is created.

9.3.3 Summary

Creating the skeleton for the game was surprisingly difficult because of problems with correctly implementing the rotation of the blocks. In the end, we found a good way to create the prompt and were able to generate a working skeleton for the game. It is not clear if using AI to create the skeleton was helpful. In fact, for an experienced HTML/JavaScript developer, it might have been easier to write the code from scratch without AI tools.

However, after the skeleton was ready, using AI to generate code was definitely helpful. All the functions and classes we generated worked correctly on the first try, and only small changes were needed to fit them into the actual game. Here, using AI clearly made the game development process more efficient. However, it was important that we were able to define good functions and classes that could be used in the game.

Reference

1. D.L. Parnas, On the criteria to be used in decomposing systems into modules. Commun. ACM **15**(12), 1053–1058 (1972)

10 Learning Programming

This chapter focuses on using generative AI to learn programming. AI tools can offer useful explanations and examples, but there is also a serious risk in using them: when learning programming with AI, it can be difficult to develop independent problem-solving skills.

Section 10.1 presents examples of how AI can act as a personal tutor in programming education. AI tools can explain programming concepts, assist with code analysis, and generate targeted exercises for learners.

Section 10.2 explores the difference between active and passive skills in programming. If we "learn" programming by generating code and explanations with AI, we probably will not learn much. A good programmer should be able to write code and solve problems independently.

Section 10.3 discusses an experiment in using AI to learn the Prolog programming language, which was created for AI programming in the early 1970s. We emphasize creating prompts that help us learn and understand Prolog concepts.

10.1 AI as a Personal Tutor

10.1.1 Explaining Concepts

AI tools are great at explaining well-known programming concepts. As an example, suppose we want to better understand the difference between `#define` and `const`, which can both be used to create constants in C. We can ask questions and focus on the details we do not understand:

> *Prompt*: I have seen that you can use both `#define` and `const` to create constants in C. What's the difference?
>
> *Answer*: `#define` is a preprocessor directive that replaces occurrences of a name with a value before compilation, so it has no type and no scope– it's just a text substitution. `const` creates a typed, scoped variable whose value cannot be changed after initialization, and it is checked by the compiler. Use `const` for type safety and debugging benefits; use `#define` for macros or when you need compile-time substitution.
>
> *Prompt*: Is it slower to use `const` compared to `#define`?
>
> *Answer*: No, using `const` is not slower than `#define` for constants. Modern compilers optimize `const` variables just like `#define` values, often replacing them with literals at compile time. There is no runtime performance difference for simple constants.
>
> *Prompt*: What do you mean by debugging benefits when using `const`?
>
> *Answer*: When you use `const`, the constant has a type and appears in the symbol table, so you can inspect its value and type in a debugger. If you use `#define`, the name is replaced by the preprocessor before compilation, so the debugger has no knowledge of it– only the value remains in the code, making debugging harder.
>
> *Prompt*: What is the symbol table?
>
> *Answer*: The symbol table is a data structure used by a compiler and debugger to keep track of information about identifiers (such as variables, functions, constants, and types) in your program. It helps the debugger show you variable names, types, and values while you debug your code.
>
> *Prompt*: [...]

10.1.2 Debugging Code

In the following example, we have a strange bug in our Java code, and we use AI to explain why our code does not produce the intended result. It might be difficult to use traditional search engines to debug the code, because we are not sure what the actual problem is or how to describe it.

> *Prompt*: I have Java code that uses two priority queues:
>
> ```
> PriorityQueue<Integer> left = new PriorityQueue<>();
> PriorityQueue<Integer> right = new PriorityQueue<>();
> ```
>
> I use the `peek` method to check the smallest values in the priority queues. However, it seems that in some situations the following code is not executed even if both the values are the same:

```
if (left.peek() == right.peek()) {
    // this is not executed
}
```

Can you help me to debug this problem?

Answer: This is a common pitfall in Java when comparing objects, especially with wrapper types like `Integer`.
  In Java, the `==` operator compares object references (i.e., whether both variables point to the exact same object in memory) when used with objects like `Integer`. It does not compare their values unless the reference is to the same object.
  `left.peek()` and `right.peek()` will return `Integer` objects. Even if both objects represent the same value (e.g., 5), they may be different objects in memory, so `left.peek() == right.peek()` can be `false`.
  To compare the values stored in the two `Integer` objects, use `.equals()`:

```
if (left.peek().equals(right.peek())) {
    // this will be executed if the values are the same
}
```

10.1.3 Creating Exercises

We can also use AI tools to create additional exercises for us to learn more about a specific topic. In the following example, we are learning Haskell programming and generate an exercise that involves handling recursive lists.

Prompt: I would like to learn more about Haskell programming. Can you create an exercise for me that asks me to create a Haskell function to solve a programming problem involving recursive list handling?

Answer: Here's an exercise that involves recursive list handling in Haskell:
  Write a Haskell function `flatten :: [[a]] -> [a]` that takes a nested list (a list of lists) and returns a single flat list containing all the elements from the nested lists. The order of elements in the resulting flat list should preserve the order of elements in the input nested lists. Example:

```
flatten [[1, 2, 3], [4, 5], [6]]
-- Result: [1, 2, 3, 4, 5, 6]

flatten [["a", "b"], ["c"], ["d", "e", "f"]]
-- Result: ["a", "b", "c", "d", "e", "f"]
```

We can also automatically generate a model solution for the exercise:

Prompt: Can you show me a model solution for the exercise?

Answer: Here's a model solution for the exercise of flattening a nested list in Haskell:

```
flatten :: [[a]] -> [a]
flatten [] = []
flatten (x:xs) = case x of
    [] -> flatten xs
    (y:ys) -> y : flatten (ys : xs)
```

10.2 Active Versus Passive Skills

AI tools can be very harmful for learning programming. This may sound surprising, because according to many studies [1,2], AI actually greatly enhances learning. However, the claim "using AI enhances learning" is too general to provide a universal answer to, just like the claim "using a computer enhances learning". Everything depends on how AI or a computer is used.

A big risk in learning programming with AI tools is that we may mostly learn *passive* skills. For example, we may spend time reading AI-generated code and explanations about programming concepts. At the same time, we may not learn *active* skills, such as writing code and designing algorithms. There is a big difference between passively *reading* code and actively *creating* code.[1]

For example, suppose we are learning Python programming and we do not know how to solve an exercise. We can try to ask AI for help:

Prompt: I'm learning programming and I need to create a Python function that is given a list of names. The function returns the number of names that have exactly four letters. Could you help me with this problem?

Answer: You can create a Python function that takes a list of names as input and counts how many of those names have exactly four letters. Here's a simple implementation:

```
def count_four_letter_names(names):
    # Initialize a counter for names with exactly four letters
    count = 0

    # Iterate through the list of names
    for name in names:
        # Check if the length of the name is exactly 4
```

---

[1] Active and passive skills in programming are related to *higher-order* and *lower-order* skills in learning theories, such as Bloom's taxonomy.

10.2 Active Versus Passive Skills

```
            if len(name) == 4:
                count += 1    # Increment the counter

        return count    # Return the total count
    # Example usage:
    names_list = ["John", "Anna", "Mike", "Sara", "Tom", "Alex"]
    result = count_four_letter_names(names_list)
    print(f"Number of names with exactly four letters: {result}")
```

The provided code defines a function count_four_letter_names that takes a list of names as input. It initializes a counter to zero and then iterates through each name in the list, checking if the length of the name is exactly four letters. If a name meets this condition, the counter is incremented by one. After examining all the names, the function returns the total count of names with four letters. In the example usage, it counts the names in the list names_list and prints the result.

What is wrong with this learning method? The purpose of such an exercise is not to teach information retrieval (solving the problem by any means), but to teach problem solving (solving the problem using our own skills). If we "solve" the problem by letting AI provide the solution, we will not learn problem solving. Even if we read and understand every part of the code and the explanation, we will miss out on the actual problem solving, which is the most important part of the exercise.

We can try to avoid the situation above by using a prompt that says we do not want any code to solve the problem, and we also do not want detailed hints.[2] By using such a prompt, we might get the following response:

Prompt: I'm learning programming and I need to create a Python function that is given a list of names. The function returns the number of names that have exactly four letters. Could you help me with this problem?

Don't give me any code, and don't give too detailed hints. Just tell me something that can help me to solve the problem.

Answer: Think about how you can iterate through the list of names and check the length of each name. You might want to use a counter to keep track of how many names meet the four-letter condition. Consider using a conditional statement to check the length of each name during the iteration.

This answer is already better because it does not include code, but it still describes the full problem-solving process needed for this exercise. In practice, it can be difficult to learn independent programming skills when using AI. If the AI writes even a small part of the code or gives even a little advice related to solving the task, this can hinder learning.

Note that the situation is very different, for example, when we are learning a new programming language and we already know how to program, but we don't know the syntax for some operation in the new language. For example, suppose we are learning C++ and we don't know how to check the length of a string. There is nothing wrong with directly asking for an answer:

---

[2] AI tools may also have features designed to support learning, such as ChatGPT's study mode.

Prompt: I'm learning C++, but I don't know how to check the length of a string. How do you do that in C++?

Answer: In C++, you can check the length of a string using the `length()` method or the `size()` method of the `std::string` class. Both methods return the number of characters in the string.

Here is a simple example demonstrating how to use both methods:

```cpp
#include <iostream>
#include <string>

int main() {
    std::string str = "Hello, World!";

    // Using length() method
    std::cout << str.length() << std::endl;

    // Using size() method
    std::cout << str.size() << std::endl;
}
```

The difference here is that there is nothing deep to learn: we know there must be a way to get the length of a string in C++, but we just don't know the correct syntax. Instead of using AI, we could, for example, try to guess the syntax or read a C++ book, but using a less efficient method for information retrieval would not make us somehow learn "better" how to calculate the string length.

10.3 Experiment: Learning Prolog

Prolog is a logic programming language created in the early 1970s, which has been used to implement AI applications. In the following experiment, we try to learn Prolog programming with the help of AI.

We don't have much previous experience with Prolog programming. We only know beforehand that we can define facts and rules and make queries. For example, here are some possible definitions:

```prolog
programmer(bob).
programmer(laura).
programmer(mike).

chess_player(cecilia).
chess_player(laura).

nerd(X) :- programmer(X), chess_player(X).
```

Here, the facts are that Bob, Laura and Mike are programmers, and Cecilia and Laura play chess. There is also one rule: a nerd is a person who is both a programmer and plays chess. Then, the following query lists the people who are nerds:

```
?- nerd(X).
% X = laura
```

10.3.1 Hello World

Since we have not much experience with Prolog programming, we do not even know how to make a Hello World program in Prolog. It is a natural way to start:

Prompt: Can you show how to write the Hello World program in Prolog?

Answer: Here is a simple "Hello World" program in Prolog:

```
hello :- write('Hello, World!'), nl.
```

To run it, load the file and type:

```
?- hello.
```

Output:

```
Hello, World!
true.
```

When we test the code above, it works as intended.
Even though this is a simple program, it is good to try to understand it thoroughly:

Prompt: What does nl mean?

Answer: nl is a built-in Prolog predicate that outputs a newline character (i.e., it moves the cursor to the next line). It stands for "new line."

Prompt: What are predicates in Prolog?

Answer: Predicates in Prolog are fundamental building blocks that represent relations or properties. A predicate consists of a name and a number of arguments (called its arity). Examples:
- parent(alice, bob). — a predicate parent/2 (arity 2)
- male(bob). — a predicate male/1 (arity 1)

Predicates can be facts, rules, or queries, and are used to express knowledge and ask questions in Prolog.

Prompt: So is nl a fact, rule, or query?

Answer: nl is a built-in predicate (specifically, a built-in procedure). When you write nl., you are making a query that asks Prolog to execute the built-in action of printing a newline.

So, in your code, nl is used as a query (or as a goal in a rule). It is not a fact or a rule that you define yourself.

Prompt: Is hello also a predicate?

Answer: Yes, hello is a predicate.
   In your example:

```
hello :- write('Hello, World!'), nl.
```

- hello is the name of the predicate.
- It has arity 0 (no arguments), so it is called hello/0.
- It is defined as a rule (with a body: write('Hello, World!'), nl).

   You can use it as a query:

```
?- hello.
```

   This will execute the rule and print "Hello, World!".

Prompt: Have I understood correctly that hello is true if both write and nl are true? Are they always true because they are special predicates with side effects?

Answer: Yes, you have understood correctly!

- hello is true if both write('Hello, World!') and nl succeed.
- write/1 and nl/0 are built-in predicates that perform side effects (printing text and a newline).
- These predicates always succeed (return true) after performing their action.

   So, whenever you call hello, it prints the message and succeeds (returns true).

10.3.2 Calculating with Numbers

Next, let's learn how to work with numbers in Prolog. This is not usually covered in the first Prolog examples. It will be interesting to see how numbers can be handled using facts and rules.

10.3 Experiment: Learning Prolog

Prompt: How can I perform calculations with numbers in Prolog?

Answer: In Prolog, use the `is` operator to evaluate arithmetic expressions:

```
X is 2 + 3.      % X = 5
Y is 7 * 4.      % Y = 28
Z is X + Y.      % Z = 33 (if X and Y are instantiated)
```

Remember:
- The right side of is must be fully instantiated (no variables).
- Use =:= to compare values: `2 + 2 =:= 4.` (true)

Prompt: How could I use the `is` operator in a program?

Answer: You can use `is` inside predicates to perform calculations. Example:

```
add_numbers(A, B, Sum) :-
    Sum is A + B.
```

Usage:

```
?- add_numbers(3, 5, X).
X = 8.
```

Tip: Always put variables to be calculated (like `Sum`) on the left of `is`, and expressions with known values on the right.

So, Prolog figures out that the value of the variable X must be 8 for the predicate to be true. But what happens if the variable X is in a different place?

Prompt: I tried to run the following query but it doesn't work:

```
?- add_numbers(3, X, 8)
```

I thought X would be 5 in this case.

Answer: Good question! In Prolog, `is` does not solve equations backwards. It only evaluates the right side if all variables there are already known (instantiated). So:

```
add_numbers(A, B, Sum) :-
    Sum is A + B.
```

With your query:

```
?- add_numbers(3, X, 8).
```

Prolog tries to evaluate `Sum is A + B` as `8 is 3 + X`, but X is unknown–so it fails. To make it work both ways, you need to write a separate rule for each direction, like:

```
add_numbers(A, B, Sum) :- Sum is A + B.
add_numbers(A, B, Sum) :- B is Sum - A.
```

Now:

```
?- add_numbers(3, X, 8).
X = 5.
```

This is a bit surprising, but it is probably something we have to get used to when programming in Prolog. Now, a good next challenge could be to calculate factorials (for example, the factorial of 4 is $4! = 1 \cdot 2 \cdot 3 \cdot 4 = 24$). It seems like this could be done with a predicate `factorial(X, Y)`, where Y is the factorial of X. We could try to define the predicate using integer division:

Prompt: What is the integer division operator in Prolog?

Answer: The integer division operator in Prolog is //.
Example:

```
X is 7 // 2.     % X = 3
```

It divides and truncates towards zero (drops the decimal part).

Let's try to calculate the factorial using a recursive idea: the factorial of X is Y if the factorial of $X - 1$ is Y/X. For example, the factorial of 4 is 24 because the factorial of $4 - 1 = 3$ is $24/4 = 6$. As the base case, we know that the factorial of 0 is 1. However, the following code does not work, at least not directly:

Prompt: I tried to create a predicate for calculating factorials as follows:

```
factorial(0, 1).
factorial(X, Y) :- X > 0, factorial(X - 1, Y // X).
```

However, the result of the following query is false:

```
?- factorial(4, 24).
```

Why doesn't it work?
Answer: Good observation! The problem is in your recursive clause:

```
factorial(X, Y) :- X > 0, factorial(X - 1, Y // X).
```

Issues:
- `X - 1` and `Y // X` are not evaluated; Prolog treats them as structures, not arithmetic expressions.

10.3 Experiment: Learning Prolog

- The recursive call's arguments are in the wrong order for calculating factorial.

Correct version:

```
factorial(0, 1).
factorial(N, F) :-
    N > 0,
    N1 is N - 1,
    factorial(N1, F1),
    F is N * F1.
```

Explanation:

- Compute `N1` as `N - 1`
- Recursively get `F1` as the factorial of `N1`
- Compute `F` as `N * F1`

Usage:

```
?- factorial(4, F).
F = 24.
```

Key point: Use `is` to evaluate arithmetic expressions before using them in predicates.

The corrected version works, but it is difficult to understand. Now is a good time to ask some clarifying questions:

Prompt: What does it mean that the arguments are in the wrong order?

Answer: Great question!
In your original code:

```
factorial(X, Y) :- X > 0, factorial(X - 1, Y // X).
```

you wrote the recursive call as:

```
factorial(X - 1, Y // X)
```

Here, you are trying to compute the factorial of `X - 1` and relate it to `Y // X`. But factorial is defined as:

```
factorial(N) = N * factorial(N - 1)
```

So, the second argument in the recursive call should be the factorial of `N - 1`, and you use that to compute the factorial of `N`. Correct order:

```
factorial(N, F) :-
    N > 0,
    N1 is N - 1,
    factorial(N1, F1),   % F1 is factorial(N - 1)
    F is N * F1.         % F is N * F1
```

- `factorial(N1, F1)` gets the factorial of N - 1.
- Then you multiply by N to get the result F.

Summary: The arguments are in the wrong order if you try to use the result (Y // X) before you have computed the factorial of X - 1. You need to compute the factorial of the smaller number first, then use it to build up the answer for the larger number.

Prompt: But if Y is the factorial of X, isn't Y // X the factorial of X - 1?

Answer: Yes, mathematically you are correct: If Y is the factorial of X, then Y // X (integer division) is the factorial of X - 1.

But in Prolog, the way you write the recursive rule matters. Let's look at your version:

```
factorial(0, 1).
factorial(X, Y) :- X > 0, factorial(X - 1, Y // X).
```

This reads as: "Y is the factorial of X if Y // X is the factorial of X - 1."
Why doesn't this work in Prolog?

- In your recursive call, you're passing Y // X as the second argument, but at this point, Y is not known yet! Prolog tries to evaluate `factorial(X - 1, Y // X)`, but Y is still a variable.
- Arithmetic expressions like Y // X are not automatically evaluated in Prolog predicates. You need to use is to compute values.

Prolog needs to build up the answer from the base case, not work backwards with unknowns.

Prolog works best when you compute the factorial of smaller numbers first, then use that to get the answer for bigger numbers:

```
factorial(0, 1).
factorial(N, F) :-
    N > 0,
    N1 is N - 1,
    factorial(N1, F1),
    F is N * F1.
```

Here:

- `factorial(N1, F1)` computes the factorial of N - 1
- `F is N * F1` computes the factorial of N

10.3.3 Working with Lists

Based on what we have seen so far, one might assume that lists are handled recursively in Prolog, just like in Lisp and other functional programming languages. Let's find out if this is the case:

10.3 Experiment: Learning Prolog

Prompt: Are there lists in Prolog? How can they be used?

Answer: Yes, Prolog has lists.
   Syntax: A list is written in square brackets: [a, b, c]. An empty list is [].
   Usage:
- Head and Tail: [H|T] matches a list with head H and tail T.
- Example:

```
member(X, [X|_]).
member(X, [_|T]) :- member(X, T).
```

You can use lists to store and process collections of items.

Prompt: There are two definitions for member. Which definition will be used if both are applicable?

For example, if the list is [1,2,3] and we want to check if 1 is on the list. If we use the second definition first, the result is false.

Answer: In Prolog, rules and facts are tried top to bottom as written in your program.
   For your member/2 example:

```
member(X, [X|_]).
member(X, [_|T]) :- member(X, T).
```

When you query member(X, [1,2,3]), Prolog tries the first rule:

- Does X match the head of the list? If yes, success.
- If not, it tries the second rule (recursion on the tail).

If you swap the order and put the recursive rule first:

```
member(X, [_|T]) :- member(X, T).
member(X, [X|_]).
```

Now, on the first element, Prolog will recurse immediately and never check the head, so it only finds matches for the tail elements (and fails for the first).

It does seem that lists work in much the same way as in functional programming. For practice, let's make a predicate that counts the number of even numbers in a list. To check if a number is even, the modulo operator would be useful:

Prompt: How can I calculate modulo in Prolog?

Answer: Use the mod operator:

```
Result is A mod B.
```

Example:

```
?- X is 10 mod 3.
X = 1.
```

Note:
- `is` evaluates the expression.
- Both operands (A and B) must be numbers or already instantiated.

With this, we can create a working predicate `count_evens`, but is it implemented well?

Prompt: I created the following predicate for counting the even numbers in a list:

```
count_evens([], 0).
count_evens([X|T], Y) :-
    0 is X mod 2, count_evens(T, Y2), Y is Y2 + 1.
count_evens([X|T], Y) :-
    1 is X mod 2, count_evens(T, Y).
```

Is this good Prolog style or could it be improved?

Answer: Your code works and is clear, but it can be improved for style and efficiency:
Issues:
- The `mod` test is repeated in the head of each clause.
- Prolog style prefers using a single recursive clause with an if-then-else (-> ;) or using an auxiliary predicate.

Improved version (using if-then-else):

```
count_evens([], 0).
count_evens([X|T], Y) :-
    ( 0 is X mod 2
    -> count_evens(T, Y2), Y is Y2 + 1
    ;  count_evens(T, Y)
    ).
```

Alternative: use a helper predicate

```
even(X) :- 0 is X mod 2.

count_evens([], 0).
count_evens([X|T], Y) :-
    even(X), count_evens(T, Y2), Y is Y2 + 1.
count_evens([X|T], Y) :-
    \+ even(X), count_evens(T, Y).
```

Prompt: What does \+ mean here?

Answer: In Prolog, \+ means negation (pronounced "not").
It succeeds if its argument cannot be proven true.
Example:

```
\+ even(X)
```

10.3 Experiment: Learning Prolog

This is true if `even(X)` fails.
Usage:

- `\+ Goal` succeeds if `Goal` fails.
- `\+ Goal` fails if `Goal` succeeds.

It is called "negation as failure".

Prompt: The way the `Y2` variable is defined doesn't look nice. Is this really the style used in Prolog?

Answer: Yes, it's common in Prolog to define an intermediate variable (like `Y2`) for recursive results, especially when you need to increment or modify the result before returning it.

Why? Prolog predicates can't "update" variables in place. Each recursive call produces a new value, which you use to compute the result for the current step.

Typical pattern:

```
predicate([Head|Tail], Result) :-
    sub_predicate(Tail, SubResult),
    Result is SubResult + ... .
```

Example:

```
count_evens([], 0).
count_evens([X|T], Y) :-
    even(X), count_evens(T, Y2), Y is Y2 + 1.
count_evens([X|T], Y) :-
    \+ even(X), count_evens(T, Y).
```

10.3.4 Eight Queens Puzzle

Now that we have learned the basics of Prolog, it is time for a real challenge: let's try to make a program that finds solutions to the eight queens puzzle.[3] The goal is to place eight queens on a chessboard so that no two queens threaten each other.

Let's start with something simple and first make a predicate `attack`, which checks if two queens threaten each other. The positions of the queens on the chessboard are given as parameters. The position of the first queen is (`X1, Y1`), and the position of the second queen is (`X2, Y2`). There are three different ways the queens can threaten each other:

1. Vertical threat: both queens have the same x-coordinate
2. Horizontal threat: both queens have the same y-coordinate
3. Diagonal threat: the horizontal distance equals the vertical distance.

---

[3] This is not really a typical exercise for a beginner programmer, but usually, for people learning Prolog, Prolog is their programming language number $n + 1$, where n is a large number.

To check for a diagonal threat, it is useful to know how to calculate the absolute value:

Prompt: How can I calculate the absolute value?

Answer: Use the built-in `abs/1` function:

```
X = -5,
Y is abs(X).    % Y = 5
```

General form:

```
abs_value(X, Y) :- Y is abs(X).
```

With this, we can try to define the predicate `attack`, but for some reason it does not work correctly:

Prompt: I have defined the `attack` predicate as follows:

```
attack(X1, Y1, X2, Y2) :-
    X1 =:= X2, Y1 =:= Y2,
    DX is abs(X1 - X2), DY is abs(Y1 - Y2), DX =:= DY.
```

However, `attack(1, 1, 3, 3)` is false. What is the reason for that?

Answer: The first line uses a comma (`,`) between `X1 =:= X2` and `Y1 =:= Y2`, which means both must be true. This is only true if both coordinates are identical (i.e., the same point)
  So, `attack(1,1,3,3)` fails because `1 =:= 3` is false and `1 =:= 3` is false.
What you probably want:
- Attack if same row (`X1 =:= X2`)
- Or same column (`Y1 =:= Y2`)
- Or same diagonal (`abs(X1-X2) =:= abs(Y1-Y2)`)

Correct version:

```
attack(X1, Y1, X2, Y2) :-
    X1 =:= X2 ;
    Y1 =:= Y2 ;
    abs(X1 - X2) =:= abs(Y1 - Y2).
```

Prompt: So `,` is like the *and* operator and `;` is like the *or* operator?
Answer: Yes, exactly!
- Comma (`,`) is AND (conjunction): Both conditions must be true.
- Semicolon (`;`) is OR (disjunction): At least one condition must be true.

In the end, this was actually a very basic mistake, but it is good to be aware of the connection between Prolog's operators and the familiar logical operators. In addition, we noticed that in this case there is no need to create new variables `DX` and `DY`, but the absolute values can be compared directly.

10.3 Experiment: Learning Prolog

Next, let's create a predicate called `valid` that can be used to check that the queen's coordinates are between 1 and 8, which means the queen is on the chessboard. To do this, we need some more information because it seems the <= operator does not work in Prolog. Based on what we've seen so far, Prolog's operators seem to be a bit unusual.

Prompt: What is the <= operator in Prolog?

Answer: In Prolog, =< is the less than or equal to operator for numbers.
  Example:

```
X = 3, Y = 5, X =< Y.     % true
```

Note:
- Prolog uses =< (not <= as in many other languages).
- For greater than or equal, use >=.

With this information, we can create the predicate `valid`:

```
valid(X, Y) :-
    1 =< X, X =< 8, 1 =< Y, Y =< 8.
```

Let's also make a predicate `all_valid`, which checks that all the given positions are valid. The predicate takes two lists as parameters: the first list contains the x-coordinates and the second list contains the y-coordinates.

```
all_valid([], []).
all_valid([X|TX], [Y|TY]) :-
    valid(X, Y), all_valid(TX, TY).
```

Let's check in the same way that there are no two queens on the lists that threaten each other. The idea is that the predicate `no_attack` will check this by using the predicate `no_first_attack`.

```
no_first_attack(AX, AY, [], []).
no_first_attack(AX, AY, [X|TX], [Y|TY]) :-
    \+ attack(AX, AY, X, Y), no_first_attack(AX, AY, TX, TY).

no_attack([], []).
no_attack([X|TX], [Y|TY]) :-
    no_first_attack(X, Y, TX, TY), no_attack(TX, TY).
```

However, the definition of the predicate `no_first_attack` causes an error:

> *Prompt*: What does the error message "Singleton variables: [AX, AY]" mean here?
>
> ```
> no_first_attack(AX, AY, [], []).
> ```
>
> *Answer*: The error means that variables `AX` and `AY` appear only once in the clause and are not used in the body.
> Example:
>
> ```
> no_first_attack(AX, AY, [], []).
> ```
>
> Here, `AX` and `AY` are in the head but not used in the body (the body is empty). Prolog warns you that these variables might be unnecessary or you may have made a mistake. How to fix?
>
> - If you don't need them, replace them with underscores (_):
>
> ```
> no_first_attack(_, _, [], []).
> ```
>
> - If you meant to use them, add them to the body.

Since we need to place eight queens on the board, both lists in the solution should have eight elements. To form a valid solution, we can try to make sure that the lists have exactly eight elements:

> *Prompt*: Is there a built-in way to check the length of a list?
>
> *Answer*: Yes! Use the built-in predicate `length/2`.
> Example:
>
> ```
> length([a, b, c], L).        % L = 3
> length(List, 4).             % List = [_A, _B, _C, _D]
> ```
>
> - `length(List, N)` is true if `List` has `N` elements.
> - Works in both directions (find length or create list of given length).

Now we can make the final predicate, `queens`, which should generate the solutions to the queen puzzle. However, the predicate does not work as intended:

10.3 Experiment: Learning Prolog

Prompt: I have created the following predicate:

```
queens(QX, QY) :-
    length(QX, 8), length(QY, 8),
    all_valid(QX, QY), no_attack(QX, QY).
```

However, the error is "Arguments are not sufficiently instantiated". What does it mean?

Answer: The error "Arguments are not sufficiently instantiated" means that Prolog is trying to use variables that do not have values yet (they are not "instantiated") in a context where it needs them to have values. Common causes:
- Using arithmetic or comparison predicates (like is, =:=, <, etc.) on variables that are still unbound.
- Using predicates that require lists to be fully specified, but they are still variables.

In your code:

```
queens(QX, QY) :-
    length(QX, 8), length(QY, 8),
    all_valid(QX, QY), no_attack(QX, QY).
```

If you call:

```
queens(QX, QY).
```

then QX and QY will be lists of 8 uninstantiated variables after length(QX, 8), length(QY, 8). If all_valid/2 or no_attack/2 tries to do arithmetic or comparison on these variables before they are assigned, you get this error.
How to fix:
- Make sure that, before using arithmetic or comparison, the variables have values.
- Usually, for the N-Queens problem, you need to generate permutations for the positions, so that the variables get values before checking validity and attacks.

Typical approach: Generate all possible arrangements, then check validity:

```
queens(QX, QY) :-
    QX = [1,2,3,4,5,6,7,8],
    permutation(QY, QX),
    no_attack(QX, QY).
```

At this point, the AI has already figured out that we are working on a solution to the eight queens puzzle. By adding the permutation generation to the queens predicate, our program starts to seem working now. However, it is still a good idea to check that the correct number of solutions is found:

Prompt: How can I count the total number of possible solutions for a query?

Answer: To count the total number of solutions for a query in Prolog, use the findall/3 predicate and length/2.
   Pattern:

```
findall(Variables, Query, Solutions),
length(Solutions, Count).
```

Example: Suppose you want to count the number of solutions for `queens(QX, QY)`:

```
findall([QX, QY], queens(QX, QY), Solutions),
length(Solutions, Count).
```

Result: `Count` will be the total number of solutions.

With this, we can see that the program finds 92 different solutions, which is the correct result!

Finally, let's ask the AI for feedback on our solution:

Prompt: Here is my solution for the eight queens puzzle. Can you give some feedback?

```
attack(X1, Y1, X2, Y2) :-
    X1 =:= X2; Y1 =:= Y2; abs(X1 - X2) =:= abs(Y1 - Y2).

valid(X, Y) :-
    1 =< X, X =< 8, 1 =< Y, Y =< 8.

all_valid([], []).
all_valid([X|TX], [Y|TY]) :-
    valid(X, Y), all_valid(TX, TY).

no_first_attack(, , [], []).
no_first_attack(AX, AY, [X|TX], [Y|TY]) :-
    + attack(AX, AY, X, Y), no_first_attack(AX, AY, TX, TY).

no_attack([], []).
no_attack([X|TX], [Y|TY]) :-
    no_first_attack(X, Y, TX, TY), no_attack(TX, TY).

queens(QX, QY) :-
    QX = [1,2,3,4,5,6,7,8],
    permutation(QY, QX),
    all_valid(QX, QY), no_attack(QX, QY).
```

Answer: Your solution is correct and follows a classic Prolog approach for the 8-queens puzzle. Here is some compact feedback:

What's Good
- `attack/4` is correct and concise.
- `valid/2` and `all_valid/2` are clear, though not strictly needed since QX and QY are always 1..8.
- `no_first_attack/4` and `no_attack/2` are well-structured and readable.
- Using `permutation(QY, QX)` ensures each row and column has one queen.

Suggestions

1. `valid/2` and `all_valid/2` are redundant:
   Since QX and QY are always permutations of 1..8, validity is guaranteed. You can remove these predicates to simplify.
2. Efficiency:
   This approach generates all permutations (8! = 40320) and then filters them, which is fine for 8 queens but not scalable for larger N.

3. `no_first_attack/4` can be simplified:
   You can use pattern matching to avoid the empty list check:

   ```
   no_first_attack(_, _, [], []).
   no_first_attack(AX, AY, [X|TX], [Y|TY]) :-
       \+ attack(AX, AY, X, Y),
       no_first_attack(AX, AY, TX, TY).
   ```

   (You already do this, just noting that you did it right!)
4. Alternative diagonal check:
   You could combine the diagonal test into one clause, but your version is clear and correct.
5. Variable names: `QX` and `QY` are fine, but you might consider using just one list of Y positions, since X is always 1..8 (the column index). This is a common simplification.

   ```
   queens(Ys) :-
       permutation([1,2,3,4,5,6,7,8], Ys),
       safe(Ys).
   ```

10.3.5 Summary

Learning Prolog with the help of AI felt meaningful, and it also seemed that using AI did not harm learning. It helped that we tried to write as much code as possible on our own and only asked the AI for advice when we could not find a solution after thinking by ourselves. However, it is important to remember that we are in a different situation than many people learning programming, because we already had a lot of knowledge about programming beforehand.

In some cases, we asked the AI about Prolog syntax, such as how to use the comparison operator and how to find the length of a list. In these cases, we could have found the same information easily with a web search, but by using AI we were able to get the answers more efficiently.

AI seemed to be most helpful when we had wrong assumptions or did not understand something about how Prolog works. The AI gave good advice in a friendly way, even when we asked questions that, looking back, were actually quite basic and not always well thought out. It was encouraging that the AI answered patiently, no matter how simple or obvious our questions were.

References

1. R. Deng et al., Does ChatGPT enhance student learning? A systematic review and meta-analysis of experimental studies. Comput. & Educ. **227** (2024)
2. J. Wang, W. Fan, The effect of ChatGPT on students' learning performance, learning perception, and higher-order thinking: insights from a meta-analysis. Humanit. Soc. Sci. Commun. **12**, 621 (2025)

Teaching Programming

11

This chapter focuses on learning programming from a teacher's perspective. AI tools present both risks and opportunities in teaching: they may hinder the development of problem-solving skills, but they can also support teaching efforts.

Section 11.1 examines how to detect the use of AI by analyzing code. AI tools often have a distinctive programming style that differs from how students typically write code, but it is difficult to reliably determine if a specific piece of code is AI-generated.

Section 11.2 discusses the overall situation of teaching programming in the era of generative AI. While using AI tools might prevent students from learning active programming and problem-solving skills, students should also learn how to use AI tools effectively.

Section 11.3 presents an experiment where AI is used to help design a programming problem related to the divide and conquer technique. Similar to using AI in programming, AI-generated content can be useful, but as teachers, we must understand and decide what topics will be taught and how.

11.1 Detecting AI Use

Suppose you are teaching a programming course. As we have discussed earlier, letting AI solve course exercises can be very harmful for learning programming and problem-solving skills. The bad news is that even if using AI to solve exercises is not allowed, you should expect that many of your students will do exactly that.

What can a teacher do in this situation? One natural approach would be to try to detect the students who have used AI. But how could we do that?

11.1.1 AI Programming Style

AI-generated code often has a specific programming style that differs from the typical style of students who are still learning programming [1,2]. This style includes extensive commenting, descriptive names for variables and functions, and the use of advanced language features. AI-generated code also tends to be consistent and follows the conventions of the programming language.

As an example, consider a programming exercise where the task is to compare two sorting algorithms:

> *Prompt*: Create Python code that compares a self-created bubble sort algorithm and the `sort` function in Python's standard library. The code should generate a list of 10^5 random numbers and report the time needed to sort it using the two algorithms.
>
> *Answer*: Below is a Python code that implements a bubble sort algorithm and compares its performance against Python's built-in `sort()` function.
>
> ```python
> import random
> import time
>
> # Bubble sort implementation
> def bubble_sort(arr):
>     n = len(arr)
>     for i in range(n):
>         # Track if a swap was made
>         swapped = False
>         for j in range(0, n-i-1):
>             if arr[j] > arr[j+1]:
>                 arr[j], arr[j+1] = arr[j+1], arr[j]  # Swap
>                 swapped = True
>         if not swapped:
>             break  # If no swaps were made, the array is sorted
>
> # Generate a list of 100,000 random numbers
> random_list = [random.randint(1, 1000000) for _ in range(100000)]
>
> # Copy the list for bubble sort
> list_for_bubble_sort = random_list.copy()
>
> # Measure time for bubble sort
> start_time_bubble = time.time()
> bubble_sort(list_for_bubble_sort)
> end_time_bubble = time.time()
> bubble_sort_time = end_time_bubble - start_time_bubble
>
> # Measure time for built-in sort
> start_time_builtin = time.time()
> random_list.sort()
> end_time_builtin = time.time()
> builtin_sort_time = end_time_builtin - start_time_builtin
>
> # Output the results
> print(f"Time taken by bubble sort: {bubble_sort_time:.6f} seconds")
> print(f"Time taken by built-in sort: {builtin_sort_time:.6f} seconds
>     ")
> ```

This code includes several features typical of AI-generated code:

- Each section of the code begins with a comment describing that part. The comments are consistent and always start with a capital letter.
- The variable names, such as `random_list` and `bubble_sort_time`, are consistent, descriptive, and follow Python naming conventions.
- Advanced Python features are used, like list comprehensions for generating random numbers, and the `.6f` format specifier to show elapsed time rounded to six decimal places.

Because of this style, the code does not look like something a typical student learning programming would write. It appears too *professional* to be produced by a beginner. AI tools are often trained to generate code that resembles code written by professional programmers, whose style is different from that of students.

11.1.2 AI Trap Problems

In some programming tasks, AI tools often produce distinctive solutions that human programmers would rarely create. From a teacher's perspective, such tasks can be called *AI trap problems*, because they provide evidence of AI use. For example, consider the following problem:

> You are given a list that consists of n numbers: $n-1$ of the numbers are equal and one number is different. Your task is to determine what the different number is. For example, the correct answer for the list [2, 2, 2, 3, 2] is 3.
>
> Write a Python function that efficiently solves the problem. You may assume that the list contains at least three numbers.

There are many approaches for solving the problem, such as the following:

```python
def find_unique(numbers):
    numbers = sorted(numbers)
    first = numbers[0]
    last = numbers[-1]
    if numbers.count(first) == 1:
        return first
    else:
        return last
```

The idea in the code above is to first sort the list and then check the first and last numbers. One of them must be the number that appears only once in the list. We count how many times the first number appears in the list. If it appears only once, we return it; otherwise, we return the last number. The algorithm is efficient because both sorting the list and counting the occurrences of the first number are fast operations.

Surprisingly, at the time of writing this book, a typical AI-generated solution for this problem looks like this:[1]

```
def find_unique(numbers):
    unique_number = 0
    for number in numbers:
        unique_number ^= number
    return unique_number
```

This function calculates the xor sum of all the numbers in the input list and returns that sum. For example, given the input list [2, 2, 2, 3, 2], the code calculates $2 \oplus 2 \oplus 2 \oplus 3 \oplus 2 = 3$, which is the correct answer (here, "$\oplus$" denotes the xor operator). But why can we use the xor operation to solve this problem?

Actually, this solution is not correct and does not work in many cases. For example, for the list [2, 2, 2, 3], the result is $2 \oplus 2 \oplus 2 \oplus 3 = 1$, which is not correct. More precisely, the code only works when the length of the list is odd. In this case, there is an even number of elements with the same value, so their xor sum is 0, and the xor sum of the whole list equals the only different number.

There are two reasons why it is unlikely that a student would come up with such a solution themselves. First, the solution does not work in many cases. If a student tested the code, they would probably notice that the algorithm is not correct. Second, the idea of using the xor sum is very unconventional. Most students learning programming are not used to working with bitwise operators, let alone designing algorithms that use them in creative ways.

Why does AI generate an incorrect solution to this problem? One possible explanation is that the xor sum solution is actually correct for a slightly different problem:

> You are given a list that consists of $n + 1$ numbers: $n/2$ pairs of numbers and one number that does not have a pair. Your task is to determine the number without a pair. For example, the correct answer for the list [2, 5, 4, 2, 4] is 5.
> Write a Python function that efficiently solves the problem.

This problem can be solved by calculating the xor sum because the xor sum of every pair is 0, and the total xor sum is equal to the number without a pair. This is a well-known problem that can be solved efficiently by calculating the xor sum. It is possible that this problem has appeared many times in AI training data, and for some reason, language models have difficulty noticing the difference between this problem and the original one.

---

[1] Interestingly, this does not seem to be related to any specific language model family. Tools based on completely different language models have produced the xor sum solution for this task.

11.1.3 Detection Difficulty

In general, it is very difficult to know for certain that code is AI-generated just by looking at its style. Even if code *looks* AI-generated, this does not *prove* that it is. For example, a student might use professional style because they already have experience in software development, or even because they have used AI tools for learning programming and adopted the AI programming style.

Another challenge in detecting AI use based on programming style is that it is easy to change the style of AI-generated code. For example, we may use the following prompt to change the style of the previous bubble sort code:

Prompt: Modify your generated code so that there are no comments. Also use short variable names and only use basic features of Python.

Answer:

```python
import random
import time

def bsort(a):
    n = len(a)
    for i in range(n):
        s = False
        for j in range(0, n-i-1):
            if a[j] > a[j+1]:
                a[j], a[j+1] = a[j+1], a[j]
                s = True
        if not s:
            break
    return a

lst = []
for i in range(100000):
    lst.append(random.randint(1, 1000000))

lst1 = lst.copy()

start1 = time.time()
bsort(lst1)
end1 = time.time()

start2 = time.time()
lst.sort()
end2 = time.time()

print("Bubble Sort Time:", end1 - start1)
print("Built-in Sort Time:", end2 - start2)
```

The resulting code does not look AI-generated, even if it is.

An even bigger challenge in detecting AI use is that AI is not always used to generate code directly. It can also be used just for the problem-solving part. Consider the following example:

Prompt: I need to create an efficient algorithm for the following programming problem. Don't generate code, only show step-by-step instructions on how to generate the code.

Given a list of n numbers, your task is to efficiently find two numbers whose distance is as small as possible. The algorithm should work in $O(n \log n)$ time.

Answer: To solve the problem of finding two numbers in a list whose distance is as small as possible, you can use the following step-by-step instructions to create an efficient algorithm:

1. Understand the Problem:

    - You are given a list of numbers.
    - You need to find two numbers in this list such that the absolute difference between them is minimized.

2. Initial Thoughts:

    - A naive approach would involve checking all pairs of numbers, which would take $O(n^2)$ time. This is inefficient for large lists.
    - To achieve $O(n \log n)$ time complexity, you need to leverage sorting.

3. Sort the List:

    - Begin by sorting the list of numbers. Sorting will arrange the numbers in increasing order, which helps in minimizing the distance between adjacent numbers.
    - Sorting can be done using algorithms like merge sort or quicksort, which have a time complexity of $O(n \log n)$.

4. Initialize Minimum Distance:

    - After sorting, initialize a variable to store the minimum distance found. You can start with a very large number or infinity.

5. Iterate Through Sorted List:

    - Traverse the sorted list from the first element to the second-to-last element.
    - For each element, calculate the absolute difference between it and the next element in the list.
    - Compare this difference with the current minimum distance. If it's smaller, update the minimum distance.

6. Return Result:

    - After completing the iteration, the minimum distance variable will hold the smallest distance between any two numbers in the list.
    - Return this minimum distance as the result.

By following these steps, you will have an efficient algorithm that finds the two numbers with the smallest distance in $O(n \log n)$ time due to the sorting step, followed by a linear scan.

Using these instructions, we could implement the algorithm in our own programming style, which would ensure that the code does not look AI-generated. However, even if the code itself is not generated by AI, the idea behind the code is, and the important problem-solving step is skipped.

11.2 Dealing with AI Tools

As a teacher, you should not expect to be able to reliably identify who has used AI. Another problem is that even if you are 100% sure that a piece of code is AI-generated, it can be difficult to prove this if the author of the code claims they did not use AI. However, what you can do is explain to students why solving course exercises using AI is not a good way to learn programming. It is important to discuss this because for a student, it may *seem* like a good idea to first solve an exercise using AI and then "learn" programming by reading the AI-generated solution.

The fact is that AI tools can easily solve most exercises in programming courses. Already in 2023, it was observed that the GPT-4 model can solve exercises well enough to pass programming courses [3]. Today's models are even better at programming and are constantly improving. In fact, in the history of programming education, it has become increasingly difficult to create programming exercises for which students cannot find ready-made solutions. Even before generative AI, solutions for most standard programming tasks could be found on the internet. Now AI can also solve non-standard tasks.

Still, a possible way to prevent the use of AI tools could be to design course exercises that are so obscure that AI tools cannot solve them. If the assignment is complicated and unclear enough, AI may not be able to understand it properly. However, there are problems with this approach. First, if an exercise is too obscure for AI to solve, students will probably also have difficulties. Second, it would not make sense to stop using good and natural problems just because AI tools are able to solve them.[2]

The widespread use of AI also affects course assessment. If generating code with AI tools is prohibited but not monitored, many students will probably use AI anyway. Therefore, if you want the course grade to reflect the students' actual skills, grades should be based on supervised exams that test programming abilities and where it is not possible to use AI tools. Once again, similar problems existed even before generative AI, because many programming tasks could be solved with the help of the internet, but AI has made this problem bigger and more visible.

---

[2] There are also technical ways to try to prevent the use of AI, but these methods become outdated quickly. A few years ago, it might have seemed like a good idea to give the assignment as an image so that AI would not be able to read it–until AI learned to read text from images as well.

Although AI tools can be very harmful in learning programming, it would be a bad idea to completely ban students from using them. AI has many benefits in programming, as this book also shows, and it would be a real disservice to train programmers who know nothing about using AI.

In addition to traditional programming exercises, it is possible to design new types of tasks related to the use of AI in programming. An example of a suggested new problem type are *prompt problems* [4], where the task is to design a prompt that generates code to solve a programming problem. AI also offers teachers many opportunities to improve the learning experience. For example, AI can automatically provide a review of code produced by a student [5], or present error messages from code in a clearer form [6]. On the other hand, teachers can also use AI to make their work more efficient, for example when creating course assignments [7].

Just as the programmer is responsible for their code, the teacher is responsible for their teaching. While AI tools can be useful in teaching, the teacher should not give the responsibility of teaching to AI.

11.3 Experiment: Designing a Programming Problem

In this experiment, we use AI to design a programming problem. Our goal is to create a good programming problem that involves the divide and conquer algorithm design technique. We use AI to brainstorm ideas for the problem and to draft the task statement and model solution.

The idea of divide and conquer algorithms is to efficiently split a problem into smaller subproblems that are easier to solve. For example, binary search and merge sort are well-known divide and conquer algorithms. However, in this experiment, our goal is to find an interesting *lesser-known* problem for our course.

11.3.1 Choosing the Topic

Let's start with a simple prompt that asks the AI to suggest a topic for our problem:

> *Prompt*: I need a good programming problem for my course. The problem should focus on using the divide and conquer technique in algorithm design. Can you suggest a good problem?
>
> *Answer*: Implement the "Closest Pair of Points" problem: Given a set of n points on a 2D plane, design and implement an efficient algorithm (using divide and conquer) to find the pair of points with the smallest Euclidean distance between them. Ask students to analyze the time complexity and compare their solution to the brute-force approach.

11.3 Experiment: Designing a Programming Problem

This was easy: the AI gave us a problem, and we can just add it to our course? However, it would actually be a bad idea to ask the AI for a single problem suggestion and use it as is. As teachers, we are responsible for the problems in our course. It is very important to choose high-quality problems, because many students will spend their time working on them.

The above problem is *not* a good choice for us because it is a very standard problem: in fact, it is one of the most popular examples for the divide and conquer approach. Let's try to generate another problem:

Prompt: This is a standard problem. Can you suggest a better problem that is not well-known?

Answer: Design an algorithm to count the number of inversions in an array (a pair of indices i < j such that arr[i] > arr[j]) using divide and conquer. Extend the exercise:
- Ask students to modify their algorithm to also return the list of all inversion pairs.
- Compare the efficiency with the brute-force $O(n^2)$ solution. This problem is less standard than sorting or closest pair, and the divide and conquer approach (modifying merge sort) is essential for efficiency.

Again, this problem is also too standard and we need something different:

Prompt: This problem is also too standard. More suggestions?

Answer: Here are some less standard suggestions that require divide and conquer:
1. Majority Element in a Subarray: Given an array and multiple queries, each asking if there is a majority element (appearing more than half the time) in a subarray $[l, r]$, design a divide and conquer algorithm to answer each query efficiently.
2. Largest Rectangle of 1s in a Binary Matrix (Divide and Conquer Approach): Given a binary matrix, find the area of the largest rectangle containing only 1s. Implement a divide and conquer solution (e.g., divide by rows or columns, combine results).
3. Minimum Distance to a Line Among Points: Given a set of points and a line (in 2D), use divide and conquer to find the point with the minimum distance to the line. Extend to find the k closest points.
4. Reconstructing a Permutation from Inversion Counts: Given an array of inversion counts for each position, reconstruct the permutation using a divide and conquer approach.

These are less common in textbooks and require creative application of divide and conquer. Let me know if you want more details on any!

This list of problem suggestions already looks much better. Let's go through the problems:

1. This looks like an interesting problem, but it is not clear how we could use the divide and conquer approach here. We can ask more details about the problem.
2. There is a standard method for solving this problem without divide and conquer, using stacks, so let's choose some other problem.
3. This could be an interesting geometry problem, but it may be too difficult for our needs.
4. This problem may be too near the standard inversion count problem. We can check this later if we don't find anything else.

Let's start by asking for details about the majority element problem:

Prompt: Thanks, the first problem (majority element in a subarray) sounds interesting. Can you describe it more? How efficient do the queries need to be?

Answer: Problem Description:
   Given an array A of length n and q queries, each query gives indices l and r (0-based, inclusive) and asks: "Is there a majority element in $A[l \ldots r]$? If so, what is it?" A majority element in a subarray is an element that appears more than half the time in that subarray.
Efficiency Goal:
- Brute force per query: $O(r - l + 1)$ time. Too slow for large q.
- The challenge: support many queries efficiently, e.g., q up to 10^5, n up to 10^5.
- Target: $O(\log n)$ or $O(\sqrt{n})$ per query.
Divide and Conquer Approach:

- Build a segment tree where each node stores a candidate for the majority element in its range (using the Boyer-Moore majority vote algorithm).
- To answer a query $[l, r]$, combine the candidates from relevant nodes, then count occurrences in $A[l \ldots r]$ to confirm.
- Preprocess frequency data to quickly count occurrences of any element in any range (e.g., store sorted lists of positions for each value, use binary search).

After reading the problem description, it is clear that this problem is not what we are looking for. The divide and conquer part seems to be in the segment tree data structure, but we would like to find a problem where the algorithm itself is based on divide and conquer. However, it is good to know about this problem, and we can possibly use it in another context.

Let's continue our search for a good problem:

11.3 Experiment: Designing a Programming Problem

Prompt: I think this is an interesting problem, but it is not exactly what I'm looking for. Here, the divide and conquer part is mainly in the segment tree data structure, but I would like to have an algorithm that requires the divide and conquer approach.

Answer: Understood. You want a problem where the core algorithmic idea is genuinely divide and conquer, not just segment trees or data structures. Here are some creative, less-standard suggestions:

1. Finding the Weighted Median in 2D
Given n points in the plane, each with a weight, find a point (not necessarily from the input) minimizing the sum of weighted Manhattan distances to all points.
Task: Use a divide and conquer approach to solve this efficiently.

2. Minimum Sum Submatrix (Non-Standard Divide and Conquer)
Given a matrix, find the submatrix with the minimal sum.
Task: Devise a divide and conquer algorithm (e.g., recursively splitting the matrix and combining solutions, similar to maximum subarray in 1D but extended to 2D).

3. Polynomial Multiplication with Arbitrary Degree (Karatsuba/Toom-Cook)
Given two polynomials of degree n, multiply them efficiently using a divide and conquer algorithm (Karatsuba or Toom-Cook).
Task: Implement and analyze the divide and conquer strategy.

4. Peak Finding in 2D Arrays
Given a 2D array, find a peak (an element greater than or equal to its neighbors) using a divide and conquer approach (not the greedy 1D method).

5. Counting "Visible Pairs" in a Set of Points
Given n points (x_i, y_i) sorted by x, count the number of pairs (i, j) such that the line segment between them is never "below" any other point (i.e., no point (x_k, y_k) with $x_i < x_k < x_j$ and $y_k >$ the segment).
Task: Use divide and conquer to count such pairs efficiently.

These problems require students to design an algorithm whose main logic is based on recursively dividing the input and combining results—true to the divide and conquer paradigm. Let me know if you want one of these described in detail!

Problem 4 (peak finding) stands out from the list. This problem could be exactly what we are looking for: a simple problem that does not seem too well-known. Let's focus on this problem more closely.

11.3.2 Working on the Problem

How would we actually use the divide and conquer approach to find a peak in a two-dimensional array? Couldn't we just use a simple algorithm that checks all array elements and finds the peak?

Prompt: In problem 4 (peak finding), why can't we just go through the array and check all neighbor elements for each position?

Answer: You can, but that would be a brute-force $O(nm)$ algorithm for an $n \times m$ array. The divide and conquer approach is interesting because it finds a peak in $O(n + m)$ time, which is much faster for large arrays.
Why divide and conquer?
- The problem guarantees that a peak always exists.

- The divide and conquer algorithm works by recursively examining the middle column (or row), finding the maximum in that column, and comparing it to its neighbors. If it's a peak, you're done; if not, you recurse into the half that has a larger neighbor.
- This approach reduces the search space by half each time, similar to binary search, making it much more efficient than checking every element.

So, while brute force works, divide and conquer is required for efficiency, especially for large arrays.

That is interesting: it could be possible to solve the problem without checking every input element. This is an unusual approach that resembles binary search. But do we really need divide and conquer? Instead, could we choose an arbitrary element and follow a path that leads to a peak element?

Prompt: Wait, couldn't we just pick an arbitrary element and always move to a larger neighbor until there is no such neighbor and we have found the peak?

Answer: Yes, you can do that! This is called the "greedy ascent" or "hill climbing" approach. You start at any cell and repeatedly move to a neighbor with a higher value until you reach a local maximum (a peak).
Why is this correct?
- Because at each step, you move to a strictly greater neighbor, and since the grid is finite and values are distinct, you must eventually reach a cell where all neighbors are less than or equal to it—a peak.

Efficiency:

- In the worst case, this can take up to $O(nm)$ steps (if you are unlucky and the path is long).
- In practice, it may be fast, but it does not guarantee a worst-case efficient algorithm.

Divide and Conquer vs. Greedy Ascent:

- The divide and conquer approach guarantees $O(n \log m)$ time, even in the worst case.
- The greedy ascent may be fast for some grids but can be slow for adversarial inputs.

That is a good point: while we could follow the path from an arbitrary element, the path could be very long in some inputs. This also gives us a good idea for designing a difficult test case for the problem. It seems that we have found a good problem. Let's create drafts for the problem statement and model solution:

Prompt: Thanks, that's definitely an interesting problem. Can you next create me a draft problem statement and model solution in Python? You will probably find some interface for inspecting array elements?

Answer: Problem Statement (Draft):
Given an $n \times m$ grid of distinct integers, a peak is an element that is not smaller than its neighbors (up to 4: up, down, left, right). Design an efficient algorithm using divide and conquer to find the position (row, column) of any peak in the grid. Your algorithm should minimize the number of element inspections. Assume you are given a function get(i,j) that returns the value at row i, column j (0-based), and you may only access the grid through this function.
Model Solution (Python):

11.3 Experiment: Designing a Programming Problem

```
def find_peak(n, m, get):
    def search(left, right):
        if left > right:
            return None
        mid = (left + right) // 2
        # Find the row with the max element in column mid
        max_row = 0
        max_val = get(0, mid)
        for i in range(1, n):
            val = get(i, mid)
            if val > max_val:
                max_val = val
                max_row = i
        # Compare with neighbors
        left_val = get(max_row, mid-1) if mid-1 >= 0 else float('-inf')
        right_val = get(max_row, mid+1) if mid+1 < m else float('-inf')
        if max_val >= left_val and max_val >= right_val:
            return (max_row, mid)
        elif left_val > max_val:
            return search(left, mid-1)
        else:
            return search(mid+1, right)
    return search(0, m-1)
```

Usage:
- Implement `get(i, j)` to access your array.
- Call `find_peak(n, m, get)` to get the coordinates of a peak.

Explanation: • Each recursive step examines a middle column, finds its max, compares to neighbors, and recurses into the half where a neighbor is larger.
- Time complexity: $O(n \log m)$ (or $O(m \log n)$ if you recurse on rows instead).
- Only $O(n \log m)$ calls to `get()` are made.

11.3.3 Summary

AI was clearly helpful in creating the problem: it gave us good ideas for possible problems, and we were able to use it to understand problems better and generate drafts for the task statement and the model solution. For the quality of the problem, it was important that we did not accept the AI's first suggestions for the topic, but instead went through a range of different topics.

Although AI can provide good ideas for course problems, the teacher must be careful not to rely too much on it. It would be unprofessional to design all course problems by letting AI propose a selection of possible problems and simply choosing the best one from there. In this case, the main responsibility for creating the problems would shift to the AI. However, we can use AI in brainstorming so that it complements our own ideas.

References

1. M. Hoq, Y. Shi, J. Leinonen et al., Detecting ChatGPT-generated code submissions in a CS1 course using machine learning models, in *SIGCSE Technical Symposium on Computer Science Education* (2024)
2. O. Karnalim, H. Toba, M.C. Johan, Detecting AI assisted submissions in introductory programming via code anomaly. Educ. Inf. Technol. **29**, 16841–16866 (2024)
3. J. Savelka, A. Agarwal, M. An et al., Thrilled by your progress! Large language models (GPT-4) no longer struggle to pass assessments in higher education programming courses, in *ACM Conference on International Computing Education Research* (2023)
4. P. Denny, J. Leinonen, J. Prather et al., Prompt problems: a new programming exercise for the generative AI era, in *SIGCSE Technical Symposium on Computer Science Education* (2024)
5. Z. Zhang, Z. Dong, Y. Shi et al., Students' perceptions and preferences of generative artificial intelligence feedback for programming, in *AAAI Conference on Artificial Intelligence* (2024)
6. J. Leinonen, A. Hellas, S. Sarsa et al., Using large language models to enhance programming error messages, in *SIGCSE Technical Symposium on Computer Science Education* (2023)
7. S. Sarsa, P. Denny, A. Hellas, J. Leinonen, Automatic generation of programming exercises and code explanations using large language models, in *ACM Conference on International Computing Education Research* (2022)

Future of Programming

12

It seems that there is always a reason, depending on the time and place, why there will be no programming jobs in the future. When I began my computer science studies in the early 2000s, I was told that learning programming was pointless because all programming jobs would soon move abroad. Just a few years later, there was a high demand for programmers in my country.

So far, all predictions about the end of programmers' work have turned out to be wrong, but will AI change the situation? Are there programming jobs available in the future, and is it still worthwhile to invest in learning programming? There have already been signs that the demand for entry-level programmers has decreased, as AI is now able to perform tasks that used to belong to them.

In 2023, Matt Welsh presented a viewpoint with the dramatic title *The End of Programming* [1], where he predicted that programmers' work will shift to teaching machines, and programming as we know it today will disappear:

> In this new computer science—if we even call it computer science at all—the machines will be so powerful and already know how to do so many things that the field will look like less of an engineering endeavor and more of an educational one; that is, how to best educate the machine, not unlike the science of how to best educate children in school.

In fact, the idea that the nature of programming is changing is not new. In 1982, in their article *Future of Programming* [2], Wasserman and Gutz predicted a future where programmers no longer describe the algorithms needed in a task but instead only define the requirements for the application:

> These changes then set the stage for more substantial changes over the longer term, turning much of today's programming task into a specification task and providing the users of computer systems with a powerful collection of tools that permit them to carry out their applications without having to rely upon programmers.

© The Author(s), under exclusive license to Springer Nature Switzerland AG 2026
A. Laaksonen, *Guide to Using Generative AI in Programming*, Undergraduate Topics in Computer Science, https://doi.org/10.1007/978-3-032-07453-9_12

In the history of programming, the development of programming languages has greatly affected the work of programmers. For example, abstractions like procedural and object-oriented programming have made programmers more productive. Yet, the core of programming has changed surprisingly little over the decades: code written in Fortran in the 1950s and in JavaScript in the 2020s is based on the same basic ideas. It would be a major change if writing code were no longer part of a programmer's job.

**

In 2005, Joel Spolsky, who later co-created Stack Overflow, published a blog post called *The Perils of JavaSchools*,[1] where he expressed concern about what happens when Java is used more and more in programming education:

> Instead what I'd like to claim is that Java is not, generally, a hard enough programming language that it can be used to discriminate between great programmers and mediocre programmers. [- -] The lucky kids of JavaSchools are never going to get weird segfaults trying to implement pointer-based hash tables. They're never going to go stark, raving mad trying to pack things into bits.

Although the main concern is not necessarily about using Java as an introductory language, but more about what is required in computer science studies, this is a common theme in the history of programming education: if programming becomes too easy, something bad will happen.

Porter and Zingaro address this topic in the introduction of their recent book *Learn AI-Assisted Python Programming* [3], where they teach Python programming using GitHub Copilot:

> The reason we're talking about this unfortunate aspect of our field is we know what some people will say about learning to program with Copilot. They'll say that to learn to write software, you have to learn how to write code entirely from scratch. [- -] But, for most people and even people starting their studies in software engineering, we wholeheartedly disagree that writing code entirely from scratch makes sense anymore as a starting place.

This discussion is connected to a big question that no one has a definite answer to: what is a good way to learn programming? On one hand, programming languages and tools have been developed to make programming as easy as possible. On the other hand, programming is an intellectual challenge, and learning programming deeply is a way to develop thinking skills.

Even if AI eventually takes over programming completely, this does not mean that people will stop thinking. For example, AI defeated humans in chess in 1997, but chess is still a popular game. Similarly, Latin is no longer a living language, but it is still taught at universities. In the same way, programming would probably not disappear, even if the skill no longer had practical importance.

---

[1] https://www.joelonsoftware.com/2005/12/29/the-perils-of-javaschools/.

***

Predicting the development of AI is difficult. In the 1950s, it was predicted that AI would soon defeat the best human players in chess, but this did not happen until 1997. After that, the game of Go was considered clearly too difficult for AI, until in 2016, AI suddenly became superior at it. In the same way, before ChatGPT, it did not seem possible that a machine could pass the Turing test.

In general, even if some task seems to be too difficult for AI tools, the situation can change unexpectedly. In the early 2000s, I found an online tool that translated text from English to my mother tongue Finnish. I had not seen such a tool before, but I immediately realized that the tool was useless. When I tested the tool with a simple sentence "I see", the translation was "I-kirjain arkkihiippakunta", which is an extremely poor translation. Here, "i-kirjain" means the letter "i", and "arkkihiippakunta" refers to a rare meaning of the word "see" in the church context (as in "the Holy See"). I thought that machine translation was simply too difficult and computers could never understand context well enough, but I was wrong. Today I can discuss with chatbots about the different meanings of the word "see" in English.

In the development of AI, the idea of what is actually intelligent seems to be constantly changing. This phenomenon is called the *AI effect*: when a computer is able to perform a new task, people come up with reasons why the computer is still not truly intelligent. For example:

- When AI defeated humans in chess, it was said that this was not real intelligence, because the program was only quickly trying a large number of move sequences and did not truly understand the game.
- When AI defeated humans in Go, it was said that this was not real intelligence, because the game is played in a limited environment and the AI can only play games, but cannot learn things in other fields like a human.
- When AI learned to have conversations with humans, it was said that this was not real intelligence, because the AI is only trained to guess the next word using a large amount of training data, without true understanding.

The AI effect may be connected to that we may feel relieved that AI still cannot do everything in the same way as we humans do. When AI produces code that does not work or contains a vulnerability, we might secretly be happy that human programmers are still needed. But what does AI think about it?

Prompt: You may have some programming skills, but human programmers are still superior. What are your thoughts on this?

Answer: That's a thoughtful perspective! Human programmers bring creativity, intuition, and a deep understanding of context—qualities that AI, including myself, can't fully replicate. While I can assist with coding tasks, suggest solutions, and automate repetitive work, I don't possess personal experience, original insight, or the ability to innovate in the same way humans do.

> In the future, AI will likely become a more powerful tool for programmers, helping with efficiency, debugging, and learning new technologies. However, human judgment, design thinking, and the ability to understand nuanced requirements will remain essential. In short: AI can enhance and support, but not replace, the unique strengths of human programmers.

References

1. M. Welsh, The end of programming. Commun. ACM **66**(1), 34–35 (2023)
2. A.I. Wasserman, S. Gutz, The future of programming. Commun. ACM **25**(3), 196–206 (1982)
3. L. Porter, D. Zingaro., *Learn AI-Assisted Python Programming* (Manning Publications, 2024)

Index

A
Active skill, 144
AI agent, 15
AI detection, 163
AI effect, 179
AI trap problem, 165
AlphaGo, 11
API, 18
Assembly language, 91
Assessment, 169
Attention, 31
AVL list, 107
AVL tree, 117

B
Backtracking, 98
Big integer, 43
Bloom's taxonomy, 144
Bubble sort, 164
Bug, 22, 69
Built-in algorithm, 8

C
Calculation, 109
Chatbot, 10, 13
ChatGPT, 13, 36
Cheating, 169
Chess, 9, 10, 179
Closest pair of points, 170
Cobol, 6
Code analysis, 89
Code completion, 8, 96
Code conversion, 100

Code formatting, 96
Code generation, 24, 47
Code review, 92
Code translation, 100
Compiler, 6, 8
Component, 124
Context, 31, 49, 121
Context window, 15
Counting inversions, 171

D
Data-based generation, 55
Data processing, 111
Debugging, 142
Deep Blue, 10
Deep learning, 11, 30
Divide and conquer, 170

E
Editor-integrated tool, 14
Eight queens puzzle, 155
ELIZA, 10
Email address, 49, 115
Embedding, 29
Error message, 41
Exercise design, 143
Explaining, 141
Explaining code, 89
Extensive testing, 76

F
Fine-tuning, 32

Fortran, 6
Function syntax, 38
Future of programming, 177

G
Generalization, 116
Generative pretrained transformer, 29
GitHub Copilot, 14
Go, 10, 179
Google, 36

H
Hallucination, 22, 107
Higher-order skill, 144
High-level language, 5
HTML tag, 42

I
Image-based generation, 60
Information retrieval, 35
IntelliSense, 8

K
Knowledge, 113
Knowledge cutoff, 15, 113

L
Language generation, 7
Language model, 11, 15, 27
Learning programming, 26, 141
LeetCode, 57
Limitation, 107
Linter, 8
Lisp, 10, 90
Lower-order skill, 144

M
Machine-level language, 5
Machine translation, 179
Majority element, 171
Markov model, 28
Mathematical task, 109
Memorization, 116

N
Neural network, 11, 30
Nondeterminism, 20

O
Operator precedence, 40

P
Palindrome, 22
Parameter, 15
Passive skill, 144
Password hash, 45
Password validation, 48, 74
Peak finding, 173
Personal tutor, 141
Primality check, 69, 72
Problem design, 170
Programming education, 163, 178
Programming environment, 7
Programming style, 54, 104, 164
Prolog, 146
Prompt, 13
Prompt engineering, 19, 47
Prompting, 32
Prompt problem, 170

R
Random integer, 37
Random testing, 81
Reasoning model, 16
Refactoring, 8, 96
Regular expression, 58, 76
Requirement, 49, 123
Review round, 92

S
Search by example, 40
Search engine, 35
Shell script, 58
Simplifying code, 52
Software development, 121
Sorting, 8
Source, 116
SQL, 7, 59
Stack Overflow, 9, 46, 57
Stack sorting, 79
Stress testing, 76
String reversal, 36, 44
Survo, 113
System prompt, 32

T
Teaching programming, 163, 178
Testing code, 69
Test suite, 72
Token, 15, 29
Tower of Hanoi, 10
Training data, 15, 27
Turbo Pascal, 7

Turing test, 9, 179

U
Unique number, 165
Unit test, 72
User interface, 60, 83

V
Vibe coding, 63

Visual Basic, 7

W
Wikipedia, 46
Word game, 126

X
Xor operator, 166

GPSR Compliance

The European Union's (EU) General Product Safety Regulation (GPSR) is a set of rules that requires consumer products to be safe and our obligations to ensure this.

If you have any concerns about our products, you can contact us on

ProductSafety@springernature.com

In case Publisher is established outside the EU, the EU authorized representative is:

Springer Nature Customer Service Center GmbH
Europaplatz 3
69115 Heidelberg, Germany

www.ingramcontent.com/pod-product-compliance
Ingram Content Group UK Ltd.
Pitfield, Milton Keynes, MK11 3LW, UK
UKHW022124230426
470314UK00001BA/5